Why *The Mor*

MW00780493

Why *The Monkees* Matter

Teenagers, Television and American Pop Culture

ROSANNE WELCH

McFarland & Company, Inc., Publishers
Jefferson, North Carolina

LIBRARY OF CONGRESS CATALOGUING-IN-PUBLICATION DATA

Names: Welch, Rosanne, author.
Title: Why the Monkees matter : teenagers, television and American
    pop culture / Rosanne Welch.
Description: Jefferson, North Carolina : McFarland & Company, Inc.,
    Publishers, 2016 | Includes bibliographical references and index.
Identifiers: LCCN 2016022504 | ISBN 9780786479238 (softcover : acid
    free paper) ∞
Subjects: LCSH: Monkees (Musical group)—History. | Popular
    culture—United States—History—20th century.
Classification: LCC ML421.M65 W45 2016 | DDC 782.42166092/2—
    dc23
LC record available at https://lccn.loc.gov/2016022504

BRITISH LIBRARY CATALOGUING DATA ARE AVAILABLE

ISBN (print) 978-0-7864-7923-8
ISBN (ebook) 978-1-4766-2602-4

On the cover: *shown from left* Davy Jones, Mike Nesmith, Micky
Dolenz, Peter Tork from *The Monkees*, 1966 (Photofest)

Printed in the United States of America

McFarland & Company, Inc., Publishers
    Box 611, Jefferson, North Carolina 28640
    www.mcfarlandpub.com

Table of Contents

Preface: I'm (Still) a Believer

This study started with writing a piece for *Written By*, the magazine of the Writers Guild of America, about the retired writing staff of *The Monkees*. Meeting this marvelous group of early television comedy writers reminded me how much they had contributed to the magic that became *The Monkees* and how much *The Monkees* had contributed to the myth and magic that became the 1960s. That first article offered a chance to prove once again that authorship belongs to the writers first, then, in no particular order, the actors and directors both in a critical studies "actor-as-text" definition and in the way actors collaborate with the writers in the creation of their characters. I disagree deeply with scholars like Aniko Bodroghkozy, who called the Monkees plastic hippies in her book *Groove Tube: Sixties Television and the Youth Rebellion*. I assert that they were actual hippies—both on the show and in their personal lives. The fact that they became so popular with 12-year-olds in 1966 may have helped lead to the further participation of those same suburban students in the various protest movements of the early 1970s when those 12-year-olds became 18—the protest for the vote for 18-year-olds; protests against the Vietnam War; protests for passage of the Equal Rights Amendment.

I think that the musical controversies, which began with the question of whether they played their own instruments on early recordings and extends to whether they belong in the Rock and Roll Hall of Fame (housed in my hometown of Cleveland, Ohio), continue to mask the real power of their existence as an Emmy-winning television program worthy of study in any critical studies context. *The Monkees* as a television show introduced young audiences to new ideas of political ideology, a new anti-military discourse and new concepts of class and feminist theory. The program raises metatextual issues of identity since the actors used their own names on the show. Though Micky Dolenz and Peter Tork, the real-life actors, were financially successful and lived in the Laurel Canyon area beside music icons John Densmore and Mama Cass Elliot, the characters of Micky and Peter lived on their own in a beach house in Malibu dreaming of success. Where did the actors end and the characters begin in the audience's mind? Why was it so hard even for other members of the entertainment business to forget that divide such that after the show's cancelation, casting directors wondered why drummer Micky Dolenz would want to audition for a role on a new pilot?

I did not come to this study as a new observer of the program. I was a fan from the beginning at the age of 6 when the show debuted on NBC and caused what I often tease was the first great choice of a childhood lived without benefit of DVR. Should I watch *The Monkees* or *Gilligan's Island*? Both aired at the same time on different channels. I used that question as the thesis to an essay when many years later I applied to film schools and am amazed at how it still resonates with others of my generation. For my students in critical studies courses that choice harkens back to an unimaginable time before VCRs or DVRs or iPads, when one had to choose between two favorite programs and wait for summer reruns to see the one they had chosen to miss.

What I'm not sure I ought to admit is that I concocted the pitch for the piece in *Written By* partly for an excuse to interview Micky Dolenz, the teen idol of my childhood. But I can tell you that the mere fact that I, a 50-year-old professional writer and academic, squealed when I hung up the phone after the interview and immediately called three or four of my oldest and best friends, attests to the power of *The Monkees* as a cultural touchstone for our generation. What makes the show even more special is that my 38-year-old cousin feels the same, having become a second-generation fan when she discovered the show being rerun on MTV for its 20th anniversary in 1986. As Rachel Maddow stated during an interview with Peter Tork, "The teenagers of the '80s learned what it was like to be teenagers in the '60s in part due to watching *Monkees* reruns on MTV." That is a tall order for what began as a simple sitcom about a struggling rock and roll band, which tells us it was never so simple as we were led to believe.

A deep study into anything can teach us much about everything. It's why we teach critical studies in the first place and what brought me to this book in the second place. A note on style, use of first names—Micky,

Davy, Peter and Mike—refers to the fictional characters and use of last names refers to the actor/musicians. The book can be used in academic settings in whole or in part, with chapters on feminism suitable for women's studies courses and chapters on identity construction appropriate for sociology courses and the whole book useful as a resource for critical studies and television history courses. But I also wrote it in honor of the fans who love the show and lived with years of teasing when the mistaken reputation of the band and the show as "plastic" kept dogging them. With this book I hope to show that those early and continuing fans all recognized the diamond in the rough from the start.

Much has been written about the Monkees, and a large amount is scattered across many books, books about the 1960s and books about the Beatles and books about teens on television and on and on. This book is the accumulation of all that information, a repository of all the Monkees mean to television and history and of all they meant to those successive generations from the 1960s to the 1980s to the 2010s who find them on television or on YouTube and fall in love with the four teens who were and are so much more than pre-fabbed creations. Chapters can be read individually based on topics of interest or in one fell swoop.

The Monkees has come to mean so many things over the years—to me and to many others who have followed their careers both together and individually. As the band members said about singing "Daydream Believer" after Jones' death, even they don't belong to themselves anymore. *The Monkees* belongs to the audience. The television network may have canceled the show but the performers made fans' dreams come true by coming back together for concerts time and again over the years.

The documentaries have all been produced, the songs have all been written. There are few new memories to be mined. What is left is the interpretation of what it all meant. That's where this book hopes to contribute to the enduring significance of *The Monkees* as a groundbreaking television program. Whether you love 'em or you hate 'em or you've never heard of them, I hope you feel you've never seen television deconstructed like this.

I must thank several people for assisting me. I'd like to thank my dear writers' group friend Mia Turner for copy-editing the manuscript and for the many hours of phone conversations dominated by my latest research discoveries. My mother, Mary Danko, for letting me watch—but more importantly talk about—the many hours of television I consumed as a child. My husband, Douglas E. Welch, sacrificed so much of our free time to my writing time and never complained. My son, Joseph Welch, became my Monkees concert seatmate and found he enjoyed their music and energy immensely, thereby bringing fandom into the millennial generation. At his first Monkees concert he learned yet another lesson the actor/musicians have taught, when he said to me, "I hope I can find a job I like so much that I'll still be doing it when I'm their age."

Introduction: Here Come The Monkees

Reaching the 50-year mark tends to grant a modicum of respect to people and things that may have been disrespected in their early days. The Hula Hoop went from a kid craze to a staple in the physical education tool box. War surplus Spam became hip when mainlanders learned it was a staple of the Hawaiian diet. This book intends to show how this 50-year charm has proven true for *The Monkees* as a television show about four struggling rock musicians in the 1960s trying to make a living by making music. Created by a group of artists—writers, actors, directors—and originally praised with an Emmy for Outstanding Comedy Series, those involved were almost immediately dismissed for their connection to the program. But it is not some unexplainable 50-year magic that makes respect for the program suddenly rematerialize. It is the ability to analyze the artistic achievements of these writers, actors and directors through a critical studies perspetive. Many of these artists earned further awards such as Emmys, Grammys and Oscars across their careers. This book allows people to critially study *The Monkees* as a program that challenged the nascent rules of a new medium and paved the way for innovation.

Television took nearly the same amount of time to climb out of the shadow of films and gain respect as both an art form and a cultural power in society and in academia. When *The Monkees* premiered in 1966 the United States was only two decades past World War II and its ascendency as a superpower. Its identity as a country was in flux as was the identity of its citizens. Their representation in the new medium of television reflected that newly forming identity. While message movies such as *Guess Who's Coming to Dinner* (written by William Rose) populated the cinemas of the early 1960s, they required the audience to choose them and pay for them, so in many instances they were preaching to choirs of like-minded believers. That left the small screen, the television screen, to do the real work of bringing uncomfortable conversations into American living rooms without warning, into places where such messages might not have been wanted, making the exposure to the message that much more potent. When deployed, this built-in ability of television to penetrate the intimacy of the viewer's home forced audiences to face rising issues such as feminism and racism that they had purposely avoided in their daily lives. Television forced families to see things they might not have chosen to see, but needed to see, such as independent women, people of color and new political perspectives. All these things appeared on *The Monkees* long before the rise of social commentary comedies such as *All in the Family.* Television also allows fantasy to come into the viewer's life, or things that seem nothing more than fantasies but become fuel for change. In her memoir, *My Beloved World,* Supreme Court Justice Sonya Sotomayor tells the story of watching *Perry Mason.* That program allowed her to fantasize about becoming a lawyer someday, by introducing her to a profession that did not exist inside her own immigrant family.[1] In the final chapter, on the cultural cachet of *The Monkees,* you will read about many a modern rock band member who came to their calling while watching Micky, Davy, Peter and Mike perform on *The Monkees.*

Countless articles and blogs over the years have focused on the largely manufactured musical controversies, overshadowing the groundbreaking effects of the television show. If mentioned in television histories at all, *The Monkees* was seen as the bastard child when discussing counterculture humor in 1960s television, behind *Laugh-In* and *The Smothers Brothers Comedy Hour,* yet they prefigured and influenced both of those programs. *The Monkees* won the Emmy for Outstanding Comedy Series of 1967 and members of the band appeared on *Laugh-In* in October 1969 to help draw their dedicated audience to the newer program. Pat Paulsen, who would become a regular on *The Smothers Brothers Comedy Hour,* appeared on *The Monkees* in 1968. Their star on the Hollywood Walk of Fame for their contribution to television via the show, not for music, is potent proof of the quality of the original product. In reviews of their reunion tours critics often note the power of the nostalgia created by the video clips from the series that play on the giant screen behind the musicians:

> It was very telling that during the entire two-hour concert performance by the Monkees Friday night at Verizon Theatre the video screen above the stage played clips of the group's famed late '60s television show, commercials for Kool Aid and Rice

Krispies, outtakes from the series, vintage musical performances and scenes from the trippy 1968 film *Head.* Even while present-day Michael Nesmith, Micky Dolenz and Peter Tork, backed by a seven-piece band, performed song after song those images provided a strong connection to the past.[2]

Studying *The Monkees* illustrates the history and evolution of the medium of television and provides a time capsule of American society at the burgeoning of the focus on youth culture that continued into the millennium generation. Sadly, the music overshadowed many of the contributions *The Monkees* writers, actors, and directors made to television history, '60s history and the life of a Ph.D. like me. This book seeks to rectify that situation, positioning the program as a groundbreaking piece of television provided to a society in flux, a product that both embraced the new order and harkened back to more traditional times. It is difficult to be of the old and the new at the same time. That tension present in *The Monkees* kept it from becoming the candy-coated look at the past that shows involving teenagers, such as *Leave It to Beaver* and *The Adventures of Ozzie and Harriet,* had already become. The actors' long hair set them apart from the older adults of the day yet verbally they brought the antics of the Marx Brothers back to life on the small screen where an aging Groucho existed merely as a stationary game show host.

With this book I hope to mirror the detailed work of music historian Andrew Sandoval in his book *The Monkees: The Day by Day Story of the '60s TV Pop Sensation* yet to focus solely on critically studying the television program. Many iconic programs of the 1960s have received scholarly attention—*Hogan's Heroes, Bewitched, Batman*—but not *The Monkees.* Not only do I think *The Monkees* deserves this kind of rigorous cultural analysis, these deep details defend my thesis that *The Monkees* is one of television's most influential programs.

Even in the beginning, the *Saturday Evening Post* considered *The Monkees* important enough as a piece of television to be given serious coverage in the January 28, 1967, issue, which also contained a cover story on sex criminals by John Kobler, a commentary on "Vietnam: Whose War?" by political analyst Stewart Alsop and a tribute to the art of writing love songs by multiple Tony Award–winning Richard Rodgers. Less than a year later Timothy Leary made the program the focus of a long rant in *Politics of Ecstasy* (1968). After a while the comparisons to the Beatles banged away at the Monkees' musical reputations, even though the *Headquarters* album remained #2 behind *Sgt. Pepper's Lonely Hearts Club Band* during the summer of 1967. Again, this involved them as a musical group, not as a telelvision show. As the focus turned more and more toward the music and the individual musicianship of each band member, it veered away from the work they did as part of the collaboration of above the line talent on the television show.

Their genesis from long-haired bad boys to family-friendly Epcot Center entertainment took decades. Originally a negative as far as parents of the day were concerned, the fact that the characters were nice boys who happened to have long hair made such hairstyles more acceptable to the mainstream. In interviews Micky Dolenz has often likened their making long hair acceptable to the way the Fonz, Henry Winkler's character on *Happy Days,* made it acceptable to wear a black leather jacket or the way Will Smith made it acceptable to be to be young, black and enjoy rap music on *The Fresh Prince of Bel Air.* This idea aligns with the ideas presented by Pete Hamill in *Why Sinatra Matters* and Christian K. Messenger in *The Godfather and American Culture: How the Corleones Became "Our Gang."* Hamill discusses how Frank Sinatra became the first Italian to be invited into people's homes by way of his voice on the records they bought, and Messenger extrapolates that idea in order to explain the way *The God-father* turned Italians from ethnic mysteries to everyday Americans. While the Monkees were the first long-haired teenagers invited into middle American homes, Dolenz' ethnicity benefited from Sinatra's success and in turn opened doors for other, more and more ethnic performers on television, as Chapter Five will cover. Also, the cloud of nostalgia makes parents today view the programs differently than their own parents did, which is why the affiliates of Antenna TV could tout the inclusion of *The Monkees* among the rest of their family-friendly fare in 2013. Despite the fact that children of the twenty-teens see the show aired in a harmless mix that continues to include *Bewitched, Mister Ed, Flipper, The Partridge Family, I Dream of Jeannie, The Patty Duke Show,* and *Dennis The Menace,* these new viewers still react to the hidden rebellion *The Monkees* represents.

Among other television programs of the period *The Monkees* is an excellent example of complete collaboration between writers, directors and actors, to be discussed further in Chapter Three, on authorship. The show makes a good subject of study because it experimented with format and style over its short 58 episodes at a time when the mantra for programs involved never changing format. A major hit like *Bonanza* ran nearly 20 years with the same plot (and a constantly tragic run of dead girlfriends) while comedies such as *The Jack Benny Show* and *The George Burns and Gracie Allen Show* also kept religiously to a set format. On *The Monkees* viewers never knew what genre story they were about to see, a fact that will be discussed in depth in Chapter Eight, on Narrative Structures. While I love the fourth-wall-breaking work of Jack Benny and George Burns and Gracie Allen and I would not want to kick any of them out of the critical studies curriculum, I think it is time to add another masterpiece of meta-textuality to the discourse. Though this book is written from an academic perspective for scholarly television viewers (and readers), the considered consumer of the medium, it is also written for the fans, to explain not what the Monkees were but what the Monkees meant.

Late 20th century popular culture and critical studies in television courses around the country recognize two ways to read television programs: as they were intended by the creators and as they were taken in by the fans. This mirror of literary analysis can be summed up in the words of writer Ralph Waldo Emerson, "Tis the good reader that makes the good book; in every book he finds passages which seem confidences or asides hidden from all else and unmistakenly meant for his ear; the profit of books is according to the sensibility of the reader; the profoundest thought or passion sleeps as in a mine, until it is discovered by an equal mind and heart." Based on that model, television programming is considered to be of quality if it delivers universal themes and makes social justice commentary while using the medium in artistically new and creative ways. Unlike literary analysis, critical studies in television analyze not the written version, but the final, filmed product since that creation of a collaborative set of artists is what the audience experienced, not any of the individual parts alone.

With *The Monkees* in particular what the writers intended is not always what the audience continues to read into each show. Amid all the slapstick and recycled vaudevillian bits there are deeper themes that spoke to teenagers then and speak now, such as the idea that fame is not a desired goal, rather making a living as an artist is the desired goal. Writing a song that meant something was a goal to the characters on *The Monkees*, not earning embarrassing amounts of money. An idea dating from the Gilded Age was being revived by the youth culture of the 1960s. Freedom and civil liberties became their new definition of the postwar American Dream, embodied in the idea of living as an artist and not marrying too young and having 2.3 kids, a job you hate, and a house in the suburbs by the age of thirty. The fact that the four characters were positive people the audience could view during what were considered chaotic and negative times helped draw fans across the decades.

Writers on *The Monkees* experimented with freedom both in the burgeoning hippie culture and in their writing. Because the actors were eventually allowed to contribute their own music to the program, the songs they chose meant something more to the characters in the show, the actors and singers who portrayed them and the audiences who continue to sing along. Also, the medium of television was new to all the artists involved. Having been on the cultural scene only since the mid–1950s, television had not been a deep part of their childhoods. Peter Tork often reminds interviewers that television was only 16 years old when the show debuted, the age of the average audience members. All of this adds layers to the critical study of the program.

One

Sweet Young Thing
Contextualizing *The Monkees* with a Short History of Teenagers on Television

Television came of age at nearly the same time the term *teenager* did, making *The Monkees* a prime example of meeting the needs of the new demographic, long before demographics became the mantra of network executives. Previously, teenage and younger children characters on television shows were largely treated as they had always been at elite dinner tables, seen and rarely heard. Certainly few stories were told from their particular perspective. For instance, while Ronnie Burns played a fictional version of himself as the son of the fictionalized versions of his parents, George Burns and Gracie Allen, on *The George Burns and Gracie Allen Show*, few episodes ever focused on his perspective. Most sitcoms had rolled over to television from family oriented radio shows with stories told largely from the parental point of view. This makes sense considering the invention of the teenager came during the decline of scripted radio programs, largely in the 1950s, which coincided with the widespread ownership of televisions. Advertisers did not miss the opportunity to use the power of this new avenue into consumers' lives. Their focus, as the focus of most of the television programs of this era, tended to be on white, middle class teenagers. The advertisers likely felt such children had more money to devote to leisure spending. Poorer teenagers and those of color more often might need jobs to help support families or had started their own families at a younger age, thereby cutting off the time they spent in their giddy teen years. Programming did not, therefore, revolve around their lives or experiences nearly so much as around what became considered the normative American teen.

In earlier eras in the United States and around the world adults considered children mature when they reached the age of thirteen. If they lived on rural farms children would have been working from even earlier ages, feeding small animals and helping with cooking, cleaning and with caring for younger siblings in the house. When industrialization hit, children who lived in urban areas began to work in factories from the age of six or seven or did piecemeal sewing work in the home to help parents meet a quota. Eventually, progressive social movements called for compulsory education. Legislation ending child labor prevailed post the Great Depression, though child labor did not end because Americans felt children needed time to mature, but rather it ended because unemployed men needed more avenues of employment. Certainly poor children continued to work while more and more middle class children began attending school together for longer periods of their lives. Then the widespread ownership of automobiles after World War II helped build the modern suburbs. Combined with the creation of consolidated high schools, this allowed neighborhood children to travel by bus to school. Soon students from different backgrounds congregated together for six to eight hours a day, creating a new kind of culture of youth involving participation in extracurricular activities like chorus and theatre and sports.

The word *teen-ager* appeared first in *Popular Science Monthly* in 1941 as a hyphenated phrase. Fathers who had survived World War II and come home to the ability to purchase homes, thanks to the G.I. Bill, wanted to enjoy the ideal life they had fought to preserve during the war. Many also used the educational benefits provided by the G.I. Bill to further their own educations and enter careers heretofore unavailable to them. With this newfound economic bounty, such parents dreamed of sending their next generation to school rather than to work. While the term *teenager* took time to settle onto the American tongue, advertisers quickly recognized that this new teenage stage of life came with new desires in terms of products and services.[1] There is a reason that goods and services such as automobiles, clothing and even music began to offer options that appealed to teenagers in the 1950s. From hot rods to the wearing of jeans outside of the workplace to the rise of rock and roll, teenagers became a newly coveted consumer to be courted. Manufacturers and advertises discovered the teenage stage of life in the 1950s in the same way that media conglomerates such as Disney and Nickelodeon discovered the lucrative market of *tweeners* (those between childhood and the teenage years) in the 1990s with programs such as *Hannah Montana* and *iCarly* and products such as Rock Band or Guitar Hero, or the many lines of makeup designed for 9- to 13-year-olds.

As the idea of teenagers grew in the American mind their reputation as a group encompassed the wide spectrum between the pristine characters embodied by Shirley Temple in *The Bachelor and the Bobby Soxer* or Sandra Dee as *Gidget* or the wild and potentially troubled teenagers such as Sidney Poitier in *Blackboard Jungle* and James Dean, Natalie Wood and Sal Mineo in *Rebel Without a Cause*. On either end, something all teenagers shared was the need to challenge the mediocre world their parents had created and change it into the future they preferred. On *The Monkees* the band members would live a romanticized view of this dream, supporting themselves on their earnings in the jobs they loved while living together sans adult supervision in a large beach house with spectacular views and quick access to the big waves and bikini-clad women. Granted this was never the dream of all American teenagers. Yet it became media's idealized dream of teenagers, one that settled so deeply for so long into the global definition of American teenagers that producer Aaron Spelling would mine it in the 1990s when he turned *Beverly Hills, 90210* into an international television sensation.

Depending on their family backgrounds, parents and teenage viewers of the late 1960s saw *The Monkees* existing on a plane anywhere between squeaky clean and troubled. Their squeaky-clean reputation came from their tame adventures, which were dictated by television standards and practices at the time. As with *That Girl* (1966–1971) no member of the opposite sex ever spent the night in the Monkees' pad with any of them and none of the Monkees ever spent the night in the home of a single woman. In fact, the only woman ever to sleep in the Monkees' pad, Rose Marie, spent a few nights as the new tenant when the band members failed to make the rent. But she was over 40 when she did so and functioned more as a maternal figure, the episode being named "Monkee Mother." Therefore, she presented no threat to virtue, though in the television landscape of the 21st century, she might now have been played as a cougar. All the other women who arrived at the pad were observed leaving the pad once a party or meeting of any kind had ended. The troubled part of the Monkees' reputation continued to come from their long hair (then still considered rebellious and dangerous), the fact that they lived without a parent on the property and the real life interviews they engaged in during the final moments of several episodes. These end-of-episode interviews involved the actor-musicians airing their opinions about long hair, the hippie culture and participating in the Sunset Boulevard riots. Those frequently raw (in terms of content, not language) conversations made some parents ban the show since they exposed younger viewers to news they might not otherwise have heard in the pre-internet world.

All teen characters that appeared in movies and television—and even perhaps books—helped lay the ground for the arrival and acceptance of the Monkees, but since *The Monkees* is a television show, focus will remain on teenage characters in that medium. Finally, this chapter refutes the negative tone of the term "plastic teenager" placed on *The Monkees* by Aniko Bodroghkozy in her work on '60s television, *Groove Tube*. In a section with the subheading, "Monkee Business," Bodroghkozy calls the Monkees plastic hippies merely because they were born on television. Plastic hippies had been referenced early in the youth movemet in articles which addressed the hoardes of unfocused teenagers who had traveled to the Sunset Strip in search of meaning to their lives, so unlike the musically driven teens who had come earlier with a purpose.[2] Those earlier, musically driven teens were the genesis of the characters on *The Monkees*, making the characters the antithesis of plastic. Bodroghkozy reads the Monkees as fake merely because they appeared on a fictional television program, forgetting that the actors, writers and producers were real people living in that real, historical period. Eric Lefcowitz, in his book *Monkee Business,* explains further: "Authenticity, or at least the appearance of it, was suddenly crucial. It didn't matter that only one member of The Byrds, Roger McGuinn, had played on 'Mr. Tambourine Man,' or that *Pet Sounds* was practically a Brian Wilson solo album even though it was credited to The Beach Boys. Those bands [...] were viewed as organic musical ventures while The Monkees and their TV show were not."[3]

Bodroghkozy does not detail whether her definition of hippie lines up with typical dictionary definitions that list unconventional appearance, long hair, the wearing of beads, and an association with a subculture involving a rejection of conventional values. By that definition, Bodroghkozy fails to take into account not only were the actors hippies in real life, the producers and directors were, as were several of the writers.[4] The truth is that, divorced of their connection to characters on a fictional television program, each actor in his own right was an authentic, mostly American teenager from various parts of the country; Nesmith (25) the too-young-married Texan; Tork (25) the Connecticut gentleman turned Greenwich

Village folksinger; Dolenz (22) the Valley boy Cruise-Nighting Californian (later glamorized in 1973 in *American Graffiti*), and Jones (22), whose English childhood offered a throwback to the 19th century teenage life of apprenticeship, first to a racing stable and then to an agent. They were all, before the show began, authentic teenagers of the 1960s. These are the original personalities that attracted the producers and eventually—and in droves—the fans. The teenage characters who had come before them laid the groundwork.

In their earliest incarnation, teens on television appeared in one of three ways: on family friendly sitcoms, on ensemble dramas and on music shows. Mirroring family sizes of the era, family sitcoms of the 1950s and 1960s generally revolved around two parents and two or three children varying in age from elementary age to junior high and early high school. Shows like *Leave it to Beaver* (1957–1963) and *The Danny Thomas Show* (1953–1964) followed this format, with the *Thomas* show being the only one with teens in the regular cast that made it into the Nielsen Top Ten consistently during its run. When the teen movie genre, which included *Palm Springs Weekend* (1963) starring Connie Stevens and Troy Donahue, and *Beach Blanket Bingo* (1965), starring Frankie Avalon and Annette Funicello, gained popularity during the early 1960s, it helped lead the way towards more teen-centric television.

In the world of dramas, adults had generally ruled the storylines with programs designed around the genres of westerns, police, lawyers and doctors. These programs, set in typical work places, focused more on the characters and their professional problems than on their home lives and personal problems. Even *77 Sunset Strip* (1958–1964) focused on the two adults as the leads, Efrem Zimbalist, Jr., and Roger Smith. This show's contribution to the world of teen drama came in the character of jive-talking, constantly hair-combing, "Kookie." Played by Edd Byrnes, the valet parking attendant often helped the detectives with their cases and has been dubbed "the first teen cult star of television."[5] Byrnes' character became so popular teen singing sensation Connie Stevens partnered with him on a song celebrating his celebrity. "Kookie, Kookie (Lend Me Your Comb)" spent 13 weeks on the Billboard Music Charts in 1959. The actor's popularity among teenagers had taken the writers by surprise. In fact, in the original pilot (written by Marion Hargrove and Roy Huggins), which ran first as a film called *Girl on the Run*, Byrnes had played a hunted serial killer, captured by the good guys. At the preview the actor proved more popular than the main stars. As Huggins remembered it, "Everyone in the audience under twenty came out, took a look at Efrem Zimbalist over here and Edd Byrnes over here. And they wanted Edd's autograph. I never saw a man so shocked, surprised, pleased, flabbergasted, in my life."[6] The writers immediately rehired Byrnes and put him in the weekly series as a new character, though one who still constantly ran a comb through his very cool, slightly long hair.

A *Monkees* connection can be made to *77 Sunset Strip* in that David Winters (director of "A Coffin Too Frequent" and "Monkees Blow Their Minds") had portrayed the original Baby John in *West Side Story* on Broadway in 1957 and then played A-rab in the film version in 1961. As a teenage actor he had appeared on *77 Sunset Strip* and another popular crime show, *Naked City*. Then Winters began his directing career on *The Monkees*, one of the newer, hipper, younger directors that the producers hired in hopes of creating a look that would attract teens to the show.

After the success of *77 Sunset Strip* other dramas experimented with creating teen characters to draw in that demographic. Judging what would qualify as cool to 14-year-old boys and girls proved difficult to network executives in their '50s and '60s. Certainly, shows like *Bonanza* (created by David Dortort) succeeded in connecting to that audience by making sure the youngest of Ben Cartwright's three sons, Little Joe (played by Michael Landon), fell into the teenage range. Landon's popularity led to his own attempt at a recording career with a 1965 appearance on *Hullabaloo* singing "I Like it Like That." While that second career never took off, Landon's teen fans helped the show stay on the air from 1959 (when Landon was actually 23) to 1973 (when he was 37 in real life, but not on the show).

In 1964 *Peyton Place* arrived as a spin-off of the film (and novel) and lasted five seasons, making new teen heartthrob Ryan O'Neal a star who would go on to film stardom in *Love Story* (1970) and *Paper Moon* (1973). On *Peyton Place* O'Neal portrayed rich high school student Rodney Harrington, who dallied between bad girl Betty or good girl Alison. Harrington eventually married a pregnant Betty, enlisted after the attack on Pearl Harbor and died in the war. In his pre–Monkee days Micky Dolenz, with his hair not yet long, but curlier and longer than the crew cuts of the good boys, appeared on *Peyton Place* as a rival to Rodney's little brother Norman. As Kitch Brunner, Dolenz played a true bad boy by drugging Norman in his first episode. In his third guest appearance Dolenz and O'Neal's

16

characters end up in a fight. Guest starring on *Place* kept Dolenz in the audiences' sights in between his child actor life on *Circus Boy* and his being cast in *The Monkees.*

Daytime soap operas from *Love Is a Many Splendored Thing* (1967) to *All My Children* (1970) to *The Young and the Restless* (1973) quickly saw the value in appealing to teenagers. Teens were the other large portion of the viewing audience likely to be home when such shows aired along with the stay-at-home mothers and grandmothers who had been soap opera's first demographic. When daytime giant *General Hospital* (1963) turned their focus more and more on teen characters, particularly Laura Vining (played by Genie Francis) their ratings rose dramatically. In her life on the show Laura killed an older lover who she found was also involved with her mother. Later she married Scotty Baldwin and then had a torrid affair with Luke Spencer that culminated in a 1981 wedding episode that garnered 30 million viewers and landed in the *TV Guide* list of "100 Most Memorable Moments in TV History."

As to sitcoms, in the later '70s and '80s shows that had begun with a focus on adults would quickly turn to teenage characters like J.J. "Dynomite" Evans on *Good Times* (1974–1979) and Alex P. Keaton of *Family Ties* (1982–1989) for success. Even *Happy Days* (1974–1984), which began as a show about Richie Cunningham asking his father for advice to help him and his friends became a show about iconic '50s teen bad boy, Arthur "The Fonz" Fonzarelli. Originally, the first sitcom to focus on the lives of teens and appear on a major network, *The Many Loves of Dobie Gillis* (1959–1963), starred Dwayne Hickman and Bob Denver. *Dobie Gillis* followed a teenage boy (Hickman) and his friends through high school, the military, and college. Denver played possibly the first beatnik on television, setting the stage for *The Monkees* to focus on the hippie culture. *Dobie Gillis* introduced audiences to future teen film idols such as Tuesday Weld and Oscar nominees such as Warren Beatty. In this way, exposure to these actors would bring *The Monkees'* audience into the adult world of late '60s and early '70s new cinema, some of which would be produced by artists involved with *The Monkees.* In 1961, Beatty's status as a teen idol would be among the first to transfer from television to film when he co-starred in *Splendor in the Grass* with reigning teen actress Natalie Wood of *Rebel Without a Cause* (1955) and *West Side Story* (1961) fame. Beatty quickly survived his teen status and became a respected leading man in *The Roman Spring of Mrs. Stone* (1961) and *Bonnie and Clyde* (1967). Later in his career he won an Oscar as best director for *Reds* (1981). Both he and Wood broke out of the teen idol reputation that still traps many other young performers, including in many ways, the actors who portrayed the Monkees.

After *Dobie Gillis,* networks turned to teens more and more, often focusing on female leads, perhaps because they appeared to be safer to allow into homes on a weekly basis. In 1963 ABC presented *The Patty Duke Show*, starring a teen actress off the Broadway stage. Patty Duke had played Helen Keller in the Broadway play *The Miracle Worker* and won an Oscar for Best Supporting Actress of 1962 for reprising the role on film. On her television show she played identical twin cousins attending high school together in Brooklyn Heights, New York complete with rock and roll music at school dances and cool cars in their driveways. In 1965 the popular novel *Gidget: The Little Girl with Big Ideas* by Frederick Kohner became a series of successful films for the teen market, which then spun off the television series *Gidget* (1965–1966) starring Sally Field. A love of surfing despite her short stature gained the lead character, Franzie, the nickname Gidget from a combination of girl and midget. The beach lifestyle the show glamorized proved a perfect precursor to *The Monkees* and their pad at the beach. Due to its connection to the original novel and the fact that Kohner functioned as a script consultant, the show took Gidget's life more seriously than is remembered by television historians today, paralleling the historical treatment of *The Monkees*. Perhaps this serious look at a girls coming of age caused the teen audience to flock to it, though being busy with homework and extracurricular activities, they didn't find the show until summer reruns. By then it had already been canceled. Some of the more controversial themes began as early as the pilot (written by Ruth Brooks Flippen) where older sister, Anne, believes Gidget is having sex with Moondoggie after reading Gidget's diary, which mentions a kiss that made her "sink into nothingness." Later, when Anne's husband starts overeating he says overeating is a sure sign of sexual starvation, quite a controversial subject for a sitcom in the 1960s. In the second episode "In God, and Nobody Else, We Trust" Gidget thinks about dating a gang member, but decides against it, not because gang members are dangerous, but because the one she knows isn't authentically bad enough to improve her good girl reputation.

Unique among this early use of teenagers on television, *The Adventures of Ozzie and Harriet* bridged the gap between using the teenagers for comedic storylines and offering their musical aspirations a larger stage. When the show moved from radio to television in 1952 the focus zeroed in on how the parents managed the lives of the two teenage sons, David and Ricky. Often Ricky would be asked to play a song. Episodes with Ricky singing tended to be highly rated, though the show itself never managed to enter the top ten in its 14 years on the air. Song choice became an issue as the elder Nelson came from the big band era and the younger embraced rock and roll, stating, "Anyone who knocks rock 'n' roll either doesn't understand it, or is prejudiced against it, or is just plain square."[7] Eventually, Ricky Nelson's recording career rivaled that of Elvis Presley in a mirror of the way The Monkees would rival The Beatles. In 1958 and 1959, while Nelson was at the height of his weekly television exposure, he had more hits than Presley, which is similar to the way the Monkees' third album, *Headquarters*, maintained the number two spot behind *Sgt. Pepper's Lonely Hearts Club Band* for most of the summer of 1967.

Teenagers and music were a natural for television, offering the music labels a place to advertise their product and the teenagers a place to see new clothing styles and dance moves to share in their own schools and neighborhoods. Many local television stations aired teenage dance shows but only a few, like the iconic *American Bandstand* (1957–1987), made it to national broadcast. During the success of *Bandstand* Clark began to experiment with other programming including spinning off *Bandstand* into *Where the Action Is* (1965–1967), a musical show with comedy skits. Paul Revere and the Raiders served as the house band performing the hits of the other bands of the day. Rather than a new format, this spin-off copied a format already tried in prime time by *Shindig* (1964–1966) and *Hullabaloo* (1965–1966). Instead of being trapped in a studio à la *Bandstand* the cast and crew of *Action* traveled around Southern California, performing in various venues for the visual stimulation. Most prime time variety shows, which were quite popular in this era, revolved around hosts who were musical artists and icons, but all the age of the parents of teens such as Andy Williams and Dean Martin (whose daughter would guest star on *The Monkees* and appear in publicity shoots as a possible romance for Davy Jones) and Liberace (who would make a cameo on *The Monkees* in "Art for Monkees' Sake.")

It wouldn't be until after *The Monkees* won its Emmy for Outstanding Comedy Series in 1967 that networks began planning and programming pilots for prime time that involved young performers singing, dancing and doing sketch comedy: *Rowan & Martin's Laugh-In* (1967–1973), *The Smothers Brothers Comedy Hour* (1967–1970), and *The Sonny and Cher Comedy Hour* (1971–1974). The irony of all of this success is that the actors on *The Monkees* had proposed bringing back their show as a variety show in its third season as they felt the silly sitcom plots of the past had grown stale. In the last few episodes of the second season, elements of variety shows seeped into the program via guest segments given over to teen cult heroes such as Frank Zappa and Tim Buckley. The network disagreed, dismissed the idea, and instead canceled the program so television history cannot report on whether such a change in format would have saved or sunk their time on the small screen.

Television history can report on how the show helped change the way youth was portrayed on television. Instrumental to making the long-haired boys acceptable to a mainstream audience was making them accessible to a mainstream audience. While many critics credit the frequent end-of-episode interviews spontaneously staged by director James Frawley, several scripted shows contributed to bringing the older audience members closer to the characters as well. First season episodes "Success Story" (written by Gerald Gardner, Dee Caruso and Bernie Orenstein) and "Monkee Mother" (written by Peter Meyerson and Bob Schlitt) stand out among them. The first involved Davy's grandfather coming to America believing that Davy had already attained success. When the opposite proves true, the grandfather demands Davy return home with him. It looks like all is lost because Grandfather demands Davy meet him at the airport that afternoon. Davy takes what he fears will be his last walk on a California beach to the tune of "I Wanna Be Free," an event that turns the song from a romantic ballad to a teen protest song. Meanwhile, the rest of the Monkees go to great lengths to keep the twosome from arriving at their departure gate on time. This proves to Grandfather that Davy has "three loyal friends here. I know I can leave you safely in their hands." In fact, Grandfather goes so far as to buy into Davy's fictional stardom by introducing him to a new companion as someone who "is quite a star, you know. He drives a Rolls."

The second episode to attempt to lure the adult audience into trusting the Monkees and deciding they were good, clean kids, "Monkee Mother," introduced Rose Marie as a new renter sharing the boys' beach house when they failed to pay the rent. As scripted, her character is given a scene alone with each of the boys and sees them through a mother's eyes, allowing the many mothers watching the show with their children to make the same connection. With Mike she comments on his poor childhood and ability to be responsible; with Micky she asks for assistance repairing a faucet; for Davy she plays matchmaker, introducing him to female English ex-patriot, and declares, "You're a good boy, Davy." Rose Marie goes so far as to declare them "all good boys" as if offering the Good Housekeeping Seal of Approval to them from a member of the parental generation. Naturally, for all of them she cooked up a motherly feast they properly thanked her for before offering to play her some music. Again, serving as the voice of the older generation, Rose Marie flatly states, "I love music. What you kids play today, that's not music." Then Peter promptly responds, "I think you're gonna like this one," and the band plays "Sometime in the Morning," perhaps one of their loveliest and softest ballads (lyrics by Gerry Goffin, music by Carole King), seemingly tailor-made for a member of the older generation. Her tacit approval of both her "boys" and their music carried weight in the older viewer demographic. So might the approval of the other guest character on "Monkee Mother," William Bramley who played Larry the Moving Man who marries Millie in the end. Bramley would have been known to adult audience members for his portrayal of Officer Krupke in the film version of *West Side Story* (1961). In a metatextual way, his approval put the Monkees on the right side of the law, making them misunderstood but good kids the way Tony in *West Side Story* is essentially a misunderstood, good kid.

Whether it was on purpose or just due to the pool of available talent in the casting world, several other, older performers appeared on *The Monkees* to help inch the adult audience along in their appreciation of the show and the younger actor/musicians. In "Monkees à la Carte" Harvey Lembeck, known to the older audience members as Eric von Zipper in the Frankie Avalon/Annette Funicello *Beach Blanket* movies of the late 1950s, portrayed Fuselli, an Italian gangster attempting to muscle in on a restaurant that employed the Monkees. Stan Freberg appeared as a CEO more interested in technology than in humanity in "Monkee vs. Machine," Carl Ballantine appeared as a stereotypical television producer in "The Audition" and Monte Landis and Vic Tayback both appeared in "Art for Monkees' Sake." Hans Conried, famous for playing the very Lebanese Uncle Tonoose on *The Danny Thomas Show* from 1955 to 1964, appeared as an aging magician in "The Monkees' Paw." In his case the blooper added to the ending of the episode undid the work of previous guest stars in that he is heard to say, "I hate these kids" in response to the madcap improvisations going on around him as he is trying to say his lines. One wonders if he called Micky's father, fellow actor George Dolenz, to report that his son was out of control and acting in a highly unprofessional manner on the set.

Finally, a note about the oft-repeated idea among scholars that the international appeal of American teen television shows began in the 1990s when *Beverly Hills, 90210* and *Baywatch* were our most popular exports. *The Monkees* played in syndication in countless countries during and after its original run on American prime time, creating fan clubs in Japan, Brazil and more than 70 other countries. More importantly, the Monkees' music allowed the actors and their version of American teenagers to travel as well. Long before the teen siblings of *90210* moved from Ohio to Beverly Hills, Davy, Micky, Mike and Peter were already living in their beach house for all the world to see.

From the days before we had a word for teenagers, youth culture in America, has developed into a global influence and industry, spawning everything from Elvis to MTV. There has not been a television season since *The Monkees* that did not air a show that catered to teenagers including *Dawson's Creek*, *Buffy the Vampire Slayer*, *Gossip Girl*, *Veronica Mars* and the appropriately titled *The Secret Life of the American Teenager* among the more recent. *The Monkees* paved the way.

Two

Look Out, Here Comes Tomorrow

Counterculture Comes to Television and Middle America

In reviewing Judy Gold's one-woman show *The Judy Show: My Life as a Sitcom* Margaret Gray wrote: "Sitcoms are the Trojan horses of cultural progress, masking profound changes with their feckless characters and dopey scenarios. They sped the acceptance of blended families, single mothers and career women among other lifestyles that once appeared to threaten the status quo."[1] Had Gray added long-haired musicians to her list of lifestyles gaining acceptance through sitcom portrayals she would have covered *The Monkees,* for in the end the sitcom was more groundbreaking than the music. Much criticism aimed at *The Monkees* focuses on the Pre-Fab Four label that had more to do with the music world than the world of television, where they were not followers but leaders, boldly going where many a sitcom about youth had not gone before. Yet over time their reputation as the musical evil-twin to the Beatles has overshadowed their reputation as a groundbreaking television comedy, which deserves to be restored.

Of more importance, *The Monkees* as a television program allowed this new counterculture ideology to sneak into the homes of middle class teens around the country by slipping jokes about President Johnson's War on Poverty and the Domino Theory of Communist Containment between their silly, vaudeville-styled adventures. Much of the anti-war, anti-authority, anti-capitalist attitude came either from the original scripts or was injected during the actors' improvisational work in rehearsals—so it came from true hippies raising the question can one be a member of the counterculture and the mainstream culture at the same time?

Through watching the show, young viewers in this largely Christian nation learned about chanting, the Lotus Sutra and the existence of Indian gurus. The evidence of the counterculture conversation *The Monkees* started is in most episodes, tucked in among so much madcap nonsense that it is easily missed—and therefore dismissed—until collected together. In fact, Tork felt that *The Monkees* "probably garnered even a larger audience for that point than The Beatles did" due to their having more exposure through television than the Fab Four.[2] Likewise, Candy Leonard, author of *Beatleness,* remembers listening to the Monkees' third album, the first where they were in control of the song choices. "I hadn't listened to 'Headquarters' in years. And when I was writing the book, I put it on and I was just blown away by how out there it was. It was very countercultural, in a sense more than 'Sgt. Pepper' in a way."[3]

Bodroghkozy might be forgiven for making the mistake of calling *The Monkees* plastic since the band members contributed to this misconception when they dismissed their early music as manufactured and unartistic. Later in their juggernaut they even dubbed themselves "tin men" in the "Ditty Diego–War Chant" song lyrics that opened their own countercultural climax, the movie *Head.* Though the song is credited to screenwriter Jack Nicholson, anecdotal history says much of the song (and the film) came from a weekend the band spent in Ojai, California, with Nicholson, their television producers Schneider and Rafelson, and an admitted amount of Frodis power.[4]

The song ends with their chant fading into the background, providing conceivably the last word on *The Monkees* from the Monkees, and even they were wrong. In interviews Micky Dolenz has often said the movie "was a deconstruction of not just *The Monkees,* but of old Hollywood. It was laying down the gauntlet of the independent filmmakers, of whom Bob Rafelson is one of them. Dennis Hopper was one and he's in the movie. Peter Fonda was one, and he's in the movie."[5] At that point in the center of the whirlwind existence of their own phenomena the actors could not be subjective about their contributions to bringing the counterculture to mainstream, middle class American teens through their exposure on a weekly television show. Someone else of their time had to do it for them.

Psychologist Timothy Leary wrote about *The Monkees* and the program's effect on the youth of the day in his seminal work, *The Politics of Ecstasy* (1968). Leary asserted that while Hollywood executives thought the actor/musicians were not "offending mom and dad and the advertisers" with their "silly, suntanned, grinning ABC TV" show, the young audience knew better and enjoyed being in on the scam. To Leary, the more manufactured and marketed the program seemed, the easier it was for the actors and writers to "use the new energies to sing the new songs and pass on the new message." Speaking specifically of the television show and not their concert performances, Leary wrote, nearly in his own chant:

> Oh, you thought that was silly teenage entertainment? Don't be fooled. While it lasted, it was a classic Sufi put on. An early Christian electronic satire. The mystic magic show. A jolly Buddha laugh at hypocrisy. At early evening kiddie-time on Monday The Monkees would rush through parody drama, burlesquing the very shows that glue mom and dad to the set during prime time. Spoofing the movies and the violence and the down heavy conflict emotion themes that fascinate the middle-aged.
>
> And woven into the fast-moving psychedelic stream of action were the prophetic, holy, challenging words. Micky was rapping quickly, dropping literary names, making scholarly references; then the sudden psychedelic switch of the reality channel. He looked straight at the camera, right into your living room and up-leveled the comedy by saying: "Pretty good talking for a long-haired weirdo, huh, Mr. and Mrs. America?"[6]

Peter Tork agreed with this take on the show. In an article in 2012 he reflected that when the program debuted in 1966, young people were feeling empowered in the United States for the first time. They saw in the characters on the program a group of teens living on their own, working at their chosen craft. "That had never happened before on television. Young adults always had a senior adult to guide them through life—the vagaries of romance, and honesty and teach them life lessons, all with a little laugh on the side. … Not The Monkees. And that reflected the political reality at the time. See, during the Eisenhower era—and before that in World War II—the American people were pretty secure that those in charge of the wheels and levers of power could be counted on for reasonable competence. They kind of knew what they were doing. Along comes the Vietnam War, and everybody knows that those guys, who by then, had taken over the wheels of power, did not know what was going on."[7]

Tork's idea can be found in the narration written by Coslough Johnson for Pat Paulsen, playing the Secretary for the Department of UFO Information in "Monkees Watch Their Feet." When Paulsen announces the "increasing evidence of the alienation of our planet" he insists, "Many of us blame our leaders. Many of our leaders blame us." Then, in describing Micky as a typical teenager Johnson wrote that Micky is "tormented by a war he must fight in a country thousands of miles away." This episode is ripe with such anti-war comments. When Paulsen tries to place blame for the existence of the aliens, he says, "They want to put the blame on teenagers. Take the war for example. Whose fault is it? Not ours. We're not fighting. It must be those crazy kids. They're the ones doing all the fighting." Finally, in explaining the only way to rid the earth of aliens, Paulsen declares, "The time has come for us to stop sticking our bayonets into each other and start sticking our bayonets into outer space."

As noted previously, the word "counterculture" encompasses more than just an anti-war activism. In the 1960s, and therefore on *The Monkees,* counterculture inclued anti-authority attitudes, anti-capitalist views, less conservative clothing styles, and even the introduction of Eastern philosophies into mainstream America. In this period before the Stonewall riots of 1969 the show managed to sneak in a mention or two of the rising gay culture. All these ideologies found themselves embedded into the daily discourse of *The Monkees* via the real life interests of the writers, actors and producers, particularly in the second season when the actors went from compliant to rebellious when it came to their costumes, hairstyles, musical choices and the edgier attitude they brought to their fourth-wall-breaking asides. The two seasons bridged a moment in American history where the country went from innocence to cynicism. This cynicism, shown by the actors, writers, and directors in the second season, matches that felt by the youth culture of the time.

> "There was something very real about the way the show plugged into the emerging '60s youth culture and, without declaring its intentions, shattered the patriarchal formulas of sitcoms such as *My Three Sons* and Father Knows Best.... The kids who were starting to watch television at that point in the '60s, they could smell that the formulas of the day were not aimed at them. They were aimed at the PTSD (post-traumatic stress disorder) victims of World War II. All of them came home with PTSD before they had a name for it, and none of them would talk about their experiences in the war," he says. "They wanted their houses to look good, and they wanted their children to look good. Kids with pot were a betrayal, because they fought for the American way, which was law and order, and they went through horrific stuff to do it." But with *The Monkees,* "at last somebody was talking to the kids, and it was a revelation. I can't tell you how many people have come up to me and said, 'It was a half-hour relief from the hell of my life every week.' We hear that almost as a refrain on a daily basis."[8]—Peter Tork

As Tork noted, the pre-teens and teens of the 1960s grew from being children of the post–World War II mindset, to young adults in a Vietnam era mindset. Dolenz and Jones dealt with receiving their draft cards and deftly side-stepping the call while songwriters Tommy Boyce and Bobby Hart became involved in the movement to gain the vote for 18-year-olds with their "LUV Means Let Us Vote" campaign. Costumes in the second season illustrated the change as the actors went from J.C. Penney-perfect, button-up uniform shirts to love beads, paisley tablecloths (as Dolenz called them) and Tork's moccasin boots. Meanwhile, Dolenz changed his hair from straight to natural afro while Nesmith's sideburns extended. Even their female guest character's costumes reflected the new era. In the two seasons, women went from babushkas as in the pilot to tie-die '70s attire in the second season.

Though the brasher, more blatant counterculture content of the show came in the second season, hints of it began as early as the pilot where the anti-authority theme first appeared as the basis for the entire plot. Written by Paul Mazursky and Larry Tucker (who came from *The Danny Kaye Show*, wrote *The Monkees* pilot and later wrote screenplays for *I Love You, Alice B. Toklas!* and *Bob & Carol & Ted & Alice*) the episode opens on a Man in the Street interview illustrating how hypocritical teenagers thought adults were. While a middle-aged man (played by Mazursky) pompously declares he would help anyone he found involved in a street fight, Peter, Micky and Mike pretend to beat on the more slightly built Davy. When Davy begs the man for help he instead runs away. A clearer comment on the older generation (just then being referred to as 'the man') might be possible, but this one certainly makes its point. After the opening credits the episode concerns the band auditioning to play at a 16th birthday party being held at a local country club by an old marine buddy of their then manager, Rudy. Of note, the manager never appeared in the rest of the series. As Peter Tork has often commented in interviews, "*The Monkees* was the only TV show about adults that did not have a senior adult on the show. So it represented a new kind of egalitarian, 'we're all in this together.' I can't tell you how many people (have) said they had half an hour of sanity every week, and that was in front of the television watching *The Monkees*. The kids felt seen. They felt here was a show about living life anyway. And I think that was a terribly important thing."[9] This lack of a parental character kept the band in charge of their own lives at a time when many American teenagers were taking that kind of control in their own lives for the first time.

When introduced to the band, the former marine Charlie Russell comments that "there's something primitive about them"—a phrase applied to many of the hippies who had turned on their parents' ideas of success via materialism and were living in more natural circumstances with other like-minded youth. The first music romp, as they came to be called by the writers, involved Davy and the 16-year-old Vanessa romantically running around a local Kiddieland with the rest of the band on hand for fun. At the end of the song "I Wanna Be Free," an ode to '60s sentiments, Vanessa lassoes Davy into taking one of those old-fashioned photos in western wedding attire. Once the band is hired for the party, the flashback dissolves into Vanessa holding Davy in handcuffs and laughing maniacally. This simple visual says much about the tensions over how young women of the 1960s were being torn between old gender-specific destinies such as marriage, and newer, freer futures, and will be addressed in Chapter Four, on feminism in *The Monkees*.

After Vanessa fails her history exam the band members help her study, but they have to smuggle her out of her father's house first. This involves deceiving an adult, which they do easily. When Vanessa passes the test, she is still upset and tells the teacher "My father is prejudiced," clearly an insult from a woman of the younger generation to her elder as many middle-class Americans were discovering their parents feared a variety of minorities who had begun pressing for their Constitutional rights. When the Monkees arrive at Vanessa's party as guests (since they lost their job playing the party) the security guard refuses to believe these longhairs have been invited onto the grounds of the elite country club and shouts them off. Mike returns to declare, "You're evil," a new idea the younger generation was forming about police and other authority figures in light of the many college and street protests of the day.

What is most important to the sale of the pilot was the idea of ending with some footage from Nesmith and Jones' original screen tests in order to familiarize the audience with the long-haired actors, making them more comfortable inviting these characters into their homes each week. However, it began the stylistic device of ending various episodes with short one-minute interviews with the actors, giving the actors a chance to share their true, non-plastic nature. Their thoughts about the political protests of the youth movement became a staple of the show's format. In Jones' screen test the question of his being a "clean kid" comes up. He says he is and that he was made to put his hair over his ears to accent its length by the producers. Nesmith's contrary nature is on display from the moment he enters the *Farmer's Daughter* set, where the screen tests were held, wearing his harmonica holster around his neck. He refuses to tell the producers a story they request. Instead, Nesmith talks about being a musician for the past two years after a long period as "a failure" so he is telling the young generation that music saved him. He admits to being out of work and wanting the series role. Nesmith ends with the hippie admonition that, "I know where it's at."

The pilot may have introduced the network to the concept of the show, but not the audience since the pilot was not the first episode to be broadcast. The audience's first taste of typical Monkee business came in "Royal Flush," written by Peter Meyerson and Robert Schlitt, which aired first on September 12, 1966. In the teaser Davy saves a young woman from drowning only to learn she is Princess Bettina and her evil Uncle Otto is out to kill her before she inherits the throne on her 18th birthday. This episode also shares the anti-authority theme of the pilot. The other frequent theme, anti-capitalism, appears in the first scene of act one. Director James Frawley framed the opening shot of Davy on the phone to include an embroidered sampler on the wall just above his right shoulder that reads, "Money Is the Root of all Evil." The sampler stayed in place—and in frequent shots—for the entire run of the series. Young audience members were being both visually and verbally carefully taught that their parents' materialism would not bring them happiness. In this episode's plot, once again, the young adults save each other from the evil adults, setting the pattern for the series. However, the two episodes with the most blatantly counterculture dialogue came from the second season, "The Devil and Peter Tork" and "Frodis Caper."

The idea that the out-of-work, financially-struggling band on the program cared more for artistic freedom and expression than they did for fame carried throughout both seasons but was especially highlighted in second season, episode "The Devil and Peter Tork." In his actor commentary for this episode Tork discussed how head writers Gerald Gardner and Dee Caruso brought actual drama to the story which made the episode, "given the parameters, given the limits ... kind of interesting." In *Hey, Hey We're the Monkees: The 30th Anniversary Documentary* produced by Rhino, Dolenz names it as his favorite episode precisely because of the "drama behind it," drama which traces back to Stephen Vincent Benet's "The Devil and Daniel Webster," which traces back to Washington Irving's "The Devil and Tom Walker," which traces back to Christopher Marlowe's "The Tragical History of Doctor Faustus" which traces back to the German legend of Faust. Each of these Faustian ties is the story of a man who sells his soul to the devil for a price. In Stephen Vincent Benét's version, Webster did so for seven years of prosperity on his farm. In Washington Irving's story Walker trades his soul for riches left behind by Captain Kidd. In Marlowe's play, Doctor Faustus exchanges his soul for 24 years of life with the devil as his servant, and in the original legend Faust exchanges his soul for a moment of true happiness.

"The Devil and Peter Tork" begins with Peter entering a pawnshop full of musical instruments. He falls in love with a harp to which the middle-aged owner, Mr. Scratch, comments, "I'm sure when you say 'love' you mean 'need and desire'—no one loves things anymore." This seems a deep insult to the younger, hippie generation as they were skipping legal marriage for the act of living together, a choice many in the older generation saw as a dismissal of love. When Peter insists he loves the harp but can't afford it, Devil/Scratch offers him a contract and Peter signs, assuming it to be on consignment. As Peter walks down the street an omniscient narrator—a film device never used before or again and actually the voice of director James Frawley—invokes the episode's theme, "Soul. Some say it is a man's heart or spirit. Certainly without it we cannot survive, for no man can live without love." Playing the harp brings fame to the fictional band on the show, demonstrated through a metatextual montage of scenes from concerts given by the actor musicians. When Devil/Scratch appears to collect Peter's soul in return for Peter's fame, Peter dismisses the fame: "When I play the harp, it makes people happy." The Devil/Scratch responds, "Money's unimportant?" because it is for him and by extrapolation for his more materialistic elder peers.

Then Peter and the band imagine what hell might be to the tune of "Salesman," a song that barely made it onto broadcast television since the network thought the song was about drug salesmen rather than capitalism. Notably, the network did not have a problem, however, with the fact that the dancing women looked like Playboy Bunny devils. When Peter's friends try to physically hold him back from the Devil/Scratch, and Davy heroically offers to go in Peter's place, Devil/Scratch rebukes them with, "Why can't you young people just accept the Devil and be done with it?" Mike insists the Devil/Scratch can't take Peter until they test the contract in court. With the snap of Mr. Scratch's fingers, they all find themselves in a courtroom with a hanging judge and a jury of convicts in front of which the long-haired musicians end up defending the Bible. Mike debunks the fact that the Devil/Scratch gave Peter anything in return for the harp because "Peter didn't want fame and fortune. All Peter wanted was just his music…. Peter loved the harp and he loved the music that came from the harp. And that was inside of him." This is a tenet of both the Greenwich Village Beat Movement and the emerging folk music movement. It placed the considered purer interests of the youth movement in a superior position to the materialism fostered by their parents' generation. Mike's entire closing argument in the case encompasses that ideology: "The power of that love was inside of Peter. It was inside of him from the first. And it was that kind of power that made Peter able to play the harp…. Don't you understand what that is, when you have that inside of you. If you love music, man. You can play music…. All it takes is just love, 'cause baby in the final analysis, love is power. That's where the power is at." Then the Devil (representing adult culture) laughs off "love" and takes Peter's power to play away. Mike urges Peter to listen to what he just said and play. "The power's inside you. Nobody can give it to you, nobody can take it away." This amounts to one of the strongest anti-capitalism, anti-authority and anti-conformity monologues ever presented on the program.

Six episodes later, in what would be the last new episode aired, *The Monkees* presented "The Frodis Caper," a treasure trove of then current counterculture messages. In several interviews Dolenz recalled the story being worked out while between camera shots on the set with assistant director Jon Anderson, so the two received Story By credit for the episode. When Dolenz asked the producers for the opportunity to write and direct, they asked him to pick a writer to work with on the teleplay. Dolenz chose David Evans, a confessed "nice boy from Kansas" and the son of a Presbyterian minister who, "never defined myself in that [counterculture] way." As Evans remembered it, "Peter [Meyerson] wanted to be counterculture very much. But it was early in the counterculture movement—that happened mostly in the early '70s. Only the themes were there in the late '60s, but the movement wasn't yet culturally dominant as it would become."[10] Despite his assertions, Evans' work co-writing "Frodis Caper" with Dolenz included some of the most outrageous examples, from referencing Marshall McLuhan to their choice of episode title. The Urban Dictionary defines Frodis as a nickname for marijuana coined by Dolenz, who remembers "it had to do with Frodo from *Lord of the Rings*. That was the time when everyone was crazy about Tolkien."[11] The word appeared often in other episodes and even had a meaning off screen when it was given to the "smoking room" provided for the actors between shots on the set. In "Frodis Caper" the word refers to the plant-based alien creature that appears to be hypnotizing humans in an attempt to take over the world.

This episode opens in the bedroom of the pad, where a rooster's crow begins a Rube Goldberg contraption which releases the needle to a record player that plays "Good Morning, Good Morning" by The Beatles. In 1968 many adults still considered the Beatles counterculture rebels so the inclusion of their long-haired music appears radical. Then Micky, Mike and Davy promptly push their ringing alarm clocks onto the floor. Peter's alarm, however, never stops because he is not in bed. Walking downstairs, the others find Peter transfixed in front of the test pattern playing on the living room television. The three, minus Peter, then visit several neighbors only to discover "this thing's got a hold of everybody," including blond-haired, clean-cut Niles. Though when Davy asks, "Has this thing got a hold of you, too?" Niles responds, "I'm always like this," blatantly referencing a mellow, marijuana-smoking state of consciousness then associated with disrespectable people but here associated with blond-haired, clean-cut Niles. Mike, Micky and Davy go to the local TV station to investigate this strange phenomena and find a stagehand equally transfixed to a set displaying an eye-shaped logo quite similar to the one used by NBC's rival network CBS.

At the station Micky, Mike and Davy are captured by the evil Wizard Glick with no one to save them except Peter. To reach him, Mike suggests using mental telepathy, which Davy calls "that psychedelic stuff" and Mike refers to as "psycho jello," a hippie phrase describing either a psychic ability, the effects of psychedelic drugs, or the lame attempt by the establishment to use hippie slang to sell products.[12] It turns out not only does Micky know how to use mental telepathy, he is in possession of a chant for this exact purpose. Here is where "Frodis Caper" takes middle-class American teens where few have gone before. In an allusion to The Beatles and their interest in Eastern spirituality, Mike asks if Micky learned the chant while studying Transcendental Meditation from an Indian mystic. Micky's one-liner about the source of his mystical chant coming from a "cereal boxtop" is just a shameless satirical jab at one of *The Monkees'* chief sponsors, Kellogg's. The chant—*nam-myoho-renge-kyo*—sounds at first like his typical gibberish dialogue (as seen last against Attila the Hun in "Devil"). However, *nam-myoho-renge-kyo* is actually a teaching from the first historical

Buddha, Siddhartha Gautama. Called The Lotus Sutra, the chant declares that all living beings, regardless of gender or intelligence, have the potential to attain Buddhahood and translates to, "the teaching of the lotus flower of the wonderful law."

Nam-myoho-renge-kyo is known as the way to awaken one's Buddha nature and tap into the deepest levels of our existence, on which our own lives and that of the universe are one.[13]

Imagine being a Buddhist in the United States watching this chant practiced on mainstream network television. Would it be weird or wonderful to see a staple of your world presented as a powerful tool toward helping your heroes? One assumes this experience is akin to Catholics hearing television characters recite the "Hail Mary" when they are in trouble, or make the sign of the cross, or sing the praises of a Hail Mary pass after a football game. Imagine being an average Christian teenager who had never been exposed to other religious ideas or practices and having the chance to hear the Lotus Sutra. This might be the most countercultural moment of the entire series and the episode is far from finished at the point where the chanting occurs. First, the chant works and draws Peter to them, though he, too, ends up a prisoner. He manages to call the police for help but before they arrive, Mike finds himself untied so he unties the rest of the band and together (as always) they capture the evil wizard and his henchmen. Here the chant is repeated as one of the Henchman offers it as a way to escape the Monkees, but the chant does not work for the villains as it worked for the heroes. However, in a nod to the theme of the adults not trusting the youth of America, when the police arrive, they assume the "weirdo" kids are the villains and they release Glick and his men. The Monkees avoid arrest by focusing the policemen's attention on TV sets in the front window of a local store, which transfix them.

Sadly, the Monkees are soon recaptured, re-escape by fooling their guard with a fake card game called "creebage," and commence to save the day by searching for the Frodis Room. Here Niles reenters the story in a waft of smoke carrying a sign reading "Frodis Room" in psychedelic colors. Niles hangs the sign on a door which Micky, Mike and Davy race through and finally find the evil eye of the Frodis plant with plans to destroy it only to have it say, "Wait, please. I am friendly." It turns out the evil Wizard Glick (a middle-aged white man) "is using my Frodis power to control men's minds through his machines." If the now empathetic Monkees can help the plant get back to its ship, it can recharge and use Frodis power to overcome Glick. As Glick and his men confront the three Monkees, the screen tells us a "Typical Monkee Romp" has begun, but this one is far from typical as it is done to the tune of "Zor and Zam." Written by brothers Bill and John Chadwick with Micky on lead vocals (appropriate for a Dolenz-penned episode) it is perhaps the most controversial of all songs played on the program. The lyrics tell the story of kings from two countries who call for a war, with the twist being the ending when the war was over before it began because no one came when the "two little kings" in charge declared war. Few better examples of anti–Vietnam war or anti-draft songs appeared on national network television. A year earlier, in 1967, CBS had censored folk singer Pete Seeger, not allowing him to sing "Waist Deep in the Big Muddy" when he guest starred on *The Smothers Brothers Comedy Hour*. The network considered the anti-war song an insult to then President Lyndon Johnson and his Vietnam War policy. After pressure from the producers, Seeger sang the song on his second appearance on the show on February 25, 1968, a month before "Frodis Caper" aired.[14]

Perhaps the sing-song nature of the music kept the censors from taking the lyrics seriously, but it is likely the young audience—facing the draft as Dolenz, Jones and Tork had—were intrigued to hear a song that seemed to suggest a better way. Finally, the episode ends with the Monkees succeeding in bringing the Frodis plant to its ship. As Glick and his men storm up the hillside they are overcome by smoke from the Frodis and fall to their knees saying, "I don't want to fight anymore. I just want to lay down on the grass and be cool." This is, clearly, the closest comment ever made on the show in reference to the existence of the drug culture, but still the softer, safer pot-smoking culture rather than the heavier, heroin culture that was to come.

While "Devil" and "Frodis" are the two most blatant examples of episodes steeped in the counterculture that was creeping into pre-teen minds around the country, several such moments were scattered throughout many individual episodes. Favorite topics for metatextual asides by the actors (some scripted, some not) included long hair, the youth culture, the anti-war movement, and drugs, mainly marijuana. Their long hair created a running gag against Disneyland, which in the 1960s had a dress code that turned men with long hair away at the entry gate. It must have been known to the actors (and writers) that Disneyland employees turned away Jim (Roger) McGuinn, founder of The Byrds, in 1964 because he wore his hair in a Beatles cut.[15]

In episodes like season two, episode ten "The Wild Monkees" as the band approaches a broken down hotel populated by elderly extras, Micky quips, "Oh a virtual Disneyland for shut-ins" and Mike responds, "No it's not, man. They won't let people with long hair into Disneyland." Later that season, in "Monstrous Monkee Mash" the band encounters several famous horror film characters, including the Wolfman. Micky comments to the hairy horror icon, "You don't get a haircut, they won't let you in Disneyland." Likewise, once Mike discovers that Micky has been transformed into a Wolfman himself, his first comment is, "You know what, you better get a haircut, man. They won't let you in Disneyland like that." The rest of the long-hair jokes centered around the way society tended to treat men with long hair. In "Monkees Mind Their Manor" (written by Coslough Johnson and directed by Tork) Mr. Friar, an English butler, comes to Malibu in search of Davy. It took a while because other neighbors, when asked if they know Davy, described him as a 'long-haired weirdo.' Mr. Friar asks what that is. Micky responds, "It's a local fish. You catch it with a sharp stick." Soon after Micky helps Mr. Friar stand up after he's fainted, Friar says, "Thank you, miss" to which Micky makes distinctly annoyed faces for a beat and moves to stab him with a drum stick until Mike stops him. In "Monkee's Paw" the magician (played by Hans Conreid) says he sold the paw "to one of these long-haired weirdos." Clearly describing a hippie style of dress he continued, "You know, high heel boots, beads." In "The Picture Frame" when Micky dresses in drag and takes the stand as his own mother he is asked if Micky could ever rob a bank. Micky's 'mother' says that would be impossible, "unless he fell in with some long-haired weirdos."

Davy had addressed the issue of long hair in a first season end-of-show interview following "Success Story" when he discussed a recent visit back to his father's home in England. Davy mentioned that people on the plane referred to him as 'Miss' and then explained that his father would not let him in the house until he had his hair cut—twice—to match his father's idea of how a young man's hair should look. Another real life discussion of long hair happened at the end of "Find the Monkees" when the director asked if they'd ever been in any fights. Davy recalled an incident in Hawaii when someone "remarked about my hair" and said he didn't mind jokes, but when people "carry on about it" he grew angry.

The director asks how they all feel when they go someplace like a restaurant and are refused service due to their hair. Peter responds that he invokes his constitutional rights and the Civil Rights Act of 1964. Then the group discusses the Sunset Strip curfew riot on November 12, 1966, at the site of Pandora's Box, at the corner of Crescent Heights and Sunset. Over a thousand young people, including emerging celebrities such as Jack Nicholson and Peter Fonda—and Dolenz according to this conversation—demonstrated against a 10:00 p.m. curfew for those under 21. Peter's friend Stephen Stills of Buffalo Springfield wrote "For What It's Worth" as a reply to the riots. And Nesmith would soon write "Daily Nightly" for the Monkees to perform on the show. In the conversation, Peter says it was a riot, involving vandalism, but Micky admits to being there and defends them as demonstrations, "but I guess a lot of journalists don't know how to spell demonstrations so they use the word riot because it only has four letters." Then Mike compares the curfew to young people being told to cut their hair. Frawley asks if Mike wants all the kids in the country to wear their hair like he does. Mike says, "I'd like to see all the kids in the country wearing their hair like they'd like to." Micky and Peter agree. Micky says that the sheriff of Los Angeles said such babysitting jobs should be taken from the police and put back in the hands of the parents. Then Peter says, "Authority goes through these vicious cycles" and Davy closes it down by admitting, "The reason I haven't spoken all this time is that it doesn't matter what I say, no one will listen to me because I'm under 21."

Youth protests, including the Sunset Strip riots, were fodder for the conversations held during the screen-testing phase of casting the program. While Nesmith and Jones' screen tests eventually appeared as tags at the end of the aired pilot, "Here Come the Monkees," Dolenz and Tork's screen tests never aired. They only became widely available with the rise of YouTube. During Dolenz screen test the producers asked about "the Wanderlust scene" and Dolenz talked about Barry McGuire and his protest song "Eve of Destruction." Dolenz quoted McGuire as saying that the song would get people to "realize where they are and then take it from there." During the interview Dolenz says, "he doesn't really do it to hang people up or to kinda cut down on blood and guts but people might think about where are we and then they'll start working on it." When asked his own opinion on McGuire's idea regarding youth protests, Dolenz replies, "I think it's groovy."

Young people were seeing themselves taken seriously and hearing about other young people on a weekly basis due to *The Monkees,* often in the program but also in those end-of-show interviews scattered across the seasons. At the end of the typically tame story of "The Monkee's Paw" the film cuts to a particularly controversial end-of-show conversation with the cast. Peter opens with, "The hippie movement is dead. It was buried in San Francisco and replaced by Free Men." Then Mike says, "That's Peter's movement. He's got six people so far." The director, Jim Frawley's voice, questions whether all the people still walking around with beads and long hair and flowers are hippies. Davy says he's got beads, but he's not a hippie. Peter argues, "You got beads? You're a hippie. You got long hair, you're a hippie." Then Peter explains that the hippie movement died "because of the bad publicity" it was receiving. "Now it's clear that every time the hippies come up with something vital and interesting, the establishment will take it over and put down the people who originated it." Peter gives as an example all the psychedelic ads appearing, things that say "Turn on to" some new product, essentially taking over the hippie culture so the hippies had to invent new words. At that point the picture fades, letting the young audience ponder Peter's idea over the closing credits. Such a conversation was not being had anywhere else on network television—and cable had yet to be invented.

The long-haired weirdo references lead to a connection with the emerging drug scene when long-hair became the visual clue to a joke involving guest star Frank Zappa in the teaser of "Monkees Blow Their Minds" (written by Meyerson). Zappa appeared costumed as Mike and Mike appeared costumed as Zappa and they interviewed each other after Zappa called *The Monkees* "this wonderful television program that has done so much for you young people out there." The introduction of Zappa into the show was its own subtle nod to the normality of smoking marijuana and the actors' comfort with the emerging drug culture. In "A Coffin Too Frequent" they are introduced to a magic pill that will bring a character back from the dead during a séance. Mike's reply: "See he gives us the pill and we believe that Elmer came back from the dead." Later, when Ruth Buzzi's character calls them angels, Peter says, "We're not angels." The editors cut to the actors dressed in angelic attire floating in clouds and cut back to Micky, who deadpans to the camera, "Now *that's* a trip." In "Monkee's Paw" Micky (as the young version of the guest character Mendrake) says, "I came all this way to find the *High* Llama. Where is he?" Mike says, "He's out back sleepin' it off." Micky says, "You don't mean?" Mike says, "That's how he got his name." Later in that episode, as they attempt to teach Micky to talk again, 'Frodis' works its way into the show among several words written on the blackboard for Micky to try to say: apple, cat, Hare Krishna, legalized wisdom, Frodis. In "Monkee Chow Mein" Mike and Davy are kicked out of a restaurant when pretending to be from the Food and Drug Administration. "That's the last time I eat in that place," Mike says. "They probably serve bad food and drugs anyway." This line did not appear in the script so it must have been improvised on set with the approval of the director. The outtakes shown after "Monkees on the Wheel" episode included a scene between Micky and Mike (still dressed in his "Monstrous Monkee Mash" mummy costume) regarding the buttons each of them is wearing. When asked what his groovy button says, Micky happily repeats, "Love is the ultimate trip." Because Mike keeps breaking down in laughter before completing the description of his own button, the scene reshoots again and again. Each time Micky completes the phrase "Love is the ultimate trip" but Mike rarely gets to finish saying "Save the Texas Prairie Chicken." While the moment seems merely to offer a rare bit of on-set humor, the repetition of the phrase on Micky's button reinforces a key tenet of hippie ideology—and also introduces the idea of 'trips' into the viewer's vocabulary.

Among all the counterculture references in the program it is clearly the anti-authority/anti-war theme that appears most frequently in *Monkees* episodes. A storyline as simple as "The Chaperone" makes an anti-war statement when it makes fun of the militaristic father playing with toy soldiers on his desk while in full uniform even though he is long retired. In "The Spy Who Came In from the Cool" the operatives of the Central Intelligence Service (C.I.S.) are such bunglers they drop their guns, which misfire, illustrating that military operatives are inept. In "Monkee Mayor" Mike confronts the current mayor about his elderly neighbors who are being evicted and the mayor compares his plan to the founding of America: "From across the shores the Pilgrims landed and found Indians. Luckily, they moved those Indians. Why, throwing people out of their homes is the American way." Freelancer Jack Winter, who went on to write for *Laverne and Shirley* (where he met Penny Marshall who would hire him to advise her during her directing of *Big*) wrote this version of the founding of America. It appeared on television via this episode of *The Monkees* in 1967, a full five years before George Carlin's 1972 rendition of "America the Beautiful," the comedy routine that would include the phrases "We really gave the Indians a fast trip across the continent, did ya notice that? … Got 'em onto an offshore island, Alcatraz, right? Off the continent completely! They had to take the island to get it! Then we kicked them off there."[16] Winter's joke also prefigures *A People's History of the United States*, first published by Howard Zinn in 1980, which used quotes from Columbus' diary to tell the story of American history from the point of view of the oppressed. Demythologizing American heroes was a radical idea to be tossing around, even for the sake of a joke, in 1967, and they continued to do it in episode after episode.

In "The Monkee's Paw" the band discovers the ultimate artist's conundrum—they cannot play until they pay their union dues, but can't pay their dues until they play. Peter's aside: "While it's true there's a great deal of moral purpose to the unions they do tend to want to stranglehold." Later in the episode, the other band members tickle Micky with feathers. Hans Conreid explains, "It's a very old method for making a subject talk." When Mike says they aren't on the right track, Conreid counters with, "I don't see why not. It works in police stations all over the world." In "Monkees in the Ring" when they hear the announcer tell the fighters in the event of a knockout to go to a neutral corner, Micky says, "I wish he'd go to the corner of Crescent Heights and Sunset" and Peter concurs, "He'd be safe." This is a second reference to the Sunset Strip curfew riots, made a year after the more lengthy end-of-show interview on "Monkees' Paw." Later in the "Ring" episode, Peter checks out the TV: "Look at that carnage. What brutality." "You watching the fight?" Micky asks. "No, the news," Peter answers. Finally, in "The Card Carrying Red Shoes" when the runaway Romanian ballerina pulls a gun on Micky he says, "Guns really never solved anything. They are not the solution to the problem. They are only a coward's way out. Wouldn't you rather talk it over than hide behind a gun?" Then, in the moment Timothy Leary referenced in his famous quote, Micky mimics dialogue from several cinematic lawmen, turns to the camera and says, "Not bad for a long-haired weirdo, huh, Mr. and Mrs. America?"

The most blatant anti-war moment in the entire series ended up in nearly the most conventional sitcom story they ever presented, "Monkee Mother." As the weekly Monkee romp fades out on "Sometime in the Morning" the scene fades up on the actors' hands playing a game of dominos. Micky asks, "What is this called?" Peter responds, "Southeast Asia" and then knocks all the dominos down to cheers from the rest of the group, clearly commenting on the Domino Theory of containing communism that caused the U.S. to enter and stay in the Vietnam War. This was particularly tender territory as three of the actors, Dolenz, Jones and Tork, managed to successfully sidestep Uncle Sam's call to serve in Vietnam.

How did such blatant references make it on air? Most of the writers felt that the studio and network executives had no idea what they meant. According to writer Treva Silverman the executives didn't get the jokes, even though, "They were all wearing love beads. While they could accessorize the accessories they never got the point."[17] Much like the network executives who didn't understand the counterculture jokes on the television program, even the most mainstream executive on their early team, Don Kirshner, didn't realize the subversive anti-war message of the first hit he chose to release under the Monkees' name, "Last Train to Clarksville," but the writers did. Who else needed "one more night together" because "I don't know if I'm ever coming home" except a newly drafted young soldier? One staff writer, Peter Meyerson, had his own draft-dodging story. "I arrived all in black, staring at my shoes. They called me out for faking it but I kept it up and they sent me home anyway. Later on, my mother got a call from a friend at the draft board who said, 'They're going to take women and children before they take your son.'"[18] In 2015 the Newseum in Washington, D.C., opened an exhibit called "Reporting Vietnam" which included a kiosk of music from the era containing 40 songs considered part of the Vietnam songbook. The curators of the exhibit placed "Last Train to Clarksville" among classics that included Marvin Gaye's "What's Goin' On?" and Pete Seeger's "Waist Deep in the Big Muddy."

Finally, countercultural comments bled into the Monkees' live concerts as well. On Monday, January 2, 1967, at their concert in Oklahoma they included "rear projected scenes of the Freedom March in Montgomery, Alabama" while Jones sang "I Wanna Be Free".[19] Likewise, on July 30, 1967, at their Wembley Stadium concert in London, Davy sang the same song, "I Wanna Be Free", in front of photos of Mick Jagger, who had recently been arrested and sentenced to three months in jail on a drug charge. In that instance, the audience booed. In his book on the history of the Monkees, Andrew Sandoval claims Mike hoped the booing was a reaction to the conviction and not to Jagger in general, not being sure what attitude a Monkees fan might have had toward drugs at that time.[20] The FBI file on the group noted that the Monkees' concert "used a device in the form of a screen set up behind the performers who played certain instruments and sang as a "combo." During the concert, subliminal messages were depicted on the screen which, in the opinion of [blanked out name] constituted "left wing innovations of a political nature." These messages and pictures were flashes of riots in Berkeley, anti-U.S. messages on the war in Vietnam, racial riots in Selma, Alabama, and similar messages which had received unfavorable response from the audience."[21] Enough of the document is blanked out so that one cannot read what constituted an unfavorable response whereas other examples show that the counterculture message arrived and thrived in *The Monkees'* audience. For instance at their Forest Hills Stadium concerts from July 14 to 16 in 1967 audience members waved posters reading "Peace" and "Love Power".[22]

Forty-five years later lifetime fans defended what they gained from the program in the many obituaries that appeared after Jones' unexpected death in 2012. Typical are these words by Diane Werts, "The Monkees really did reflect societal trends, despite their fancifully simplistic TV plots. Just look at the show. Season 1 episodes have the boys—and they did seem to be "boys," despite being in their 20s—wearing tidy matching outfits, with trendy longish hair, yes, but definitely clean and polite. In Season 2, Micky's 'do has grown out into a naturally curly mop, sideburns are stretching down toward chins, and—heavens!—they're wearing tie-dyes and dashiki! Those sweet heartthrob Monkees were, dare we say it, suddenly, sort of, almost *dangerous*."[23] Even Bob Dylan, parodied in an early episode, said, "I've always believed that the first rule of being subversive is not to let anybody know you're being subversive" in reference to *Clarksville*.[24] The problem with such subtlety is that it can—and often has—been missed. Yet the inclusion of such new ideas not only brought those ideas to middle America, but in doing so *The Monkees* created a cultural time capsule of the era for each successive generation of viewers of the reruns. Political commentator Rachel Maddow referenced this idea while interviewing Tork on her program after Jones' death. She said the teenagers of the '80s learned what it was like to be teenagers in the '60s in part due to watching *Monkees* reruns on MTV and further, called the program "foundational to my American culture DNA."[25]

Clearly, the performers and the program were counterculture when counterculture was not cool with capitalist corporate-owner Colgems. The voices of the actors and the writers that came together in creating the program were diverse and similar at the same time, with one foot in the future but the other stubbornly planted back in the past. It was an inevitable position for anyone living at the fringe of the newer, freer culture that would come in the 1970s. The Monkees bridged that gap for the creators and for the audience. They may have called themselves Tin Men but these Tin Men had no need to search for heart. They wore it on their sleeves in every episode. The audience responded to that honesty despite its being trapped inside a manufacturer's plastic packaging.

Three

Words
Who Wrote the Episodes and What Was That Something They Had to Say?

The discussion of authorship in film and television creates continuous controversy in both the professional entertainment and the academic worlds. Readers regularly assume that the writer of a novel deserves full credit for his or her work despite the known assistance of editors, yet film and television viewers seem to be less willing to grant the screenwriter as much credit. The explanation for this disparity traces back to the *politique des auteurs* or the "auteur theory" with respect to directors being the sole authors of a film.[1] In the 1950s the French film critics, including François Truffaut before he became a director, created this concept in film analysis. They felt that French screenwriters wielded too much power over directors who were in many ways collaborators on dialogue and plot points. When Truffaut's films became popular in America so too did his writings in the French film magazine *Cahiers du Cinéma*. This auteur concept minimized the role of screenwriters, sometimes relegating the script to the status of a blueprint in architecture, thus further problematizing the difficulty the average audience member has had comprehending more than the work of directing and acting.

Few American film critics argued against this auteur concept until 1970 when Richard Corliss edited *The Hollywood Screenwriters: A Film Comment Book*. After detailing the elements of style and tone that belonged to the bodies of work of individual writers, Corliss wrote, "at this point in film criticism, it may be necessary to treat the screenwriter as an auteur who, through detailed script indications of camera placement, cutting, and acting styles, virtually 'directs' his own films. It is no more absurd than to argue that the director writes his own scripts." He concludes

43

by deciding that, "these two contradictory forces must be seen as complimentary, with the best Hollywood films resulting from the productive intersection of a strong writer and a strong director—and often a strong actor."[2] Later, in 1996 Stanley Cavell wrote that he attached directors' names to films as a simplistic way of identifying them and admitted that, "intention and control remain seriously under-analyzed concepts in these contexts; that my allusion to a director's intention leave its exercise wide open to investigation."[3]

The Monkees makes an excellent case study for authorship credit returning to the writers since producers Bert Schneider and Bob Rafelson never wrote for *The Monkees* as they were not writers. Meanwhile, Paul Mazursky and Larry Tucker wrote the pilot, which began to create the characters and concepts that other writers followed and honed. Since those two writers only authored the pilot, this show, as it is remembered by the fans, was written by its writing staff with some dialogue improvised by the actors on the set during filming. This aspect of authorship and this set of writers have not been featured prominently in any other books about the program, partly because public relations focused on the actors and their improvisational spontaneity, which created a long-held myth that a majority of the mayhem was made up on set. Comparisons between final drafts and aired episodes indicate that writers introduced much frivolity on the page. *The Monkees*, then, might be one of our best examples of a true triumvirate of television talent. As actor/musician Micky Dolenz remembers, it all began with the writers: "People don't appreciate how valuable and important the writers of the show were. We always had a finely crafted script with a story, a struggle, Davy falling in love with girl and getting her out of trouble. Great comedy has some sort of solid story underneath it. And then the humor, as part of the design, was not topical or satirical—so it didn't date."[4]

Bernie Orenstein, who wrote three episodes during his summer hiatus from *The Hollywood Palace*, remembers, "We certainly gave them a framework in which to improvise so more of the improv came in the physical comedy than the verbal."[5] The evidence that writers were the authors of many of the comedic moments comes from an insider's knowledge of television production that understands certain things had to be called for in the script in order for them to be available on set. For instance, in "Dance, Monkees, Dance" Orenstein wrote a comic scene where, in need of 'a brilliant idea' Micky says, "I've gotta go talk to the writers." He then breaks the fourth wall, something the cameramen had to anticipate in order to track, walks off the set into a door marked Writer's Room, where he finds a group of elderly Chinese laundry men, who had to have been cast earlier in the week. Micky says the line as it appears in the script, asking for "something fast and groovy and hip, you know, can you do it?" The fake writers type frantically on their old Underwoods which were called for in the script and procured by the property department. Micky brings the pages past the cameramen, back onto the set to the other band members mumbling, "Man, this is terrible. Those guys are really overpaid." Clearly, the scene had to be blocked, the cameras set, the fake writers cast, etc. In this case, as spontaneous as it may appear, the writer is the author of this scene.

Similarly, Coslough Johnson came to the show from a freelance episode of *Bewitched* and would go on to earn six Emmy nominations and win one for *Laugh-In*. Johnson conceived the idea of a scene where Mike enters a quiet, elegant room to find the famous pianist Liberace preparing for a performance in "Art for Monkees' Sake." That required casting Liberace and set dressing his recital room, including providing a sledgehammer as a prop. The comedy comes from subverting the expected. Rather than play the piano, Liberace destroys his piano with the sledgehammer. This makes Johnson the author of that scene. Yet within the same episode Johnson recalled that Tork made a camera aside that Johnson had not written. As the young musicians bemoan the dilemma of not being able to perform until they pay their union dues, yet not being able to pay their union dues unless they perform, Peter says, "While it's true there's a great deal of moral purpose to the unions they do tend to want to stranglehold." Even in an interview conducted fifty years later, Johnson knew he would never have written a line like that because, "I love my union. Residuals are the reason I got to retire at 65 and enjoy my retirement."[6]

Orenstein and Johnson are part of the team of writers hired by Schneider and Rafelson after the pilot sold to NBC. Therefore, what Timothy Leary defined in *The Politics of Ecstasy* as, "a classic Sci-Fi put on. An early-Christian electronic satire. A mystic magic show. A jolly Buddha laugh at hypocrisy" was honed and sustained not by producers but by an eclectic mix of writing talent representing a cross-section of youth and experience; a still-largely New York and Jewish brand of humor schooled in vaudeville and Yiddish theatre; with a collection of conservative and counterculture mindsets. The contribution of these writers has been minimized due to the enormity of film success gained by Schneider, Rafelson, Mazursky, and Tucker in their later film careers. Yet the staff writers credited with most of the original scripts on *The Monkees* have credits as stellar in television, including future Emmy Award winners, several future show creators, a humor consultant and speechwriter for Senator Robert Kennedy. Dolenz also co-wrote and directed what became the last episode and used it as a springboard to a career behind the camera creating, producing and directing English television programs until the anniversary concert tours came calling in the 1980s.

Each writer came to the show through different channels and with different backgrounds. The writer with the most episodic credits, Gerald Gardner (22 of 58), came after working on the 1964 Robert Kennedy senatorial campaign. He served as head writer, who in today's television parlance would be referred to as the show runner since he oversaw the development and rewrites of all the scripts each season. That makes his contribution larger in many ways than Mazursky's and Tucker's. Gardner began his career writing political satire in his multi-book series *Who's in Charge?* One of the books caught President John Kennedy's interest and he invited the young writer to the White House where Gardner also met Attorney General Robert Kennedy. After the assassination, a condolence letter led to Gardner being invited to bring his brand of humor to what RFK knew would be a tough campaign for the Senate seat in New York. When Kennedy won the seat, Gardner moved on to earn an Emmy nomination as part of the 1965 staff of *That Was the Week That Was.* There he met Buck Henry, who acted in and wrote for *Week.* Henry was developing *Get Smart* at the time and invited Gardner to partner with another *Week* writer, Dee Caruso and come out to the West Coast where many television shows were relocating.[7] After they had written a few episodes, Rafelson approached Henry looking for funny young writers for his own new show. Henry recommended Gardner and Caruso. Gardner recalled, "Both *Get Smart* and *The Monkees* were influenced by British comedy and culture. *Get Smart* was a send off of the whole James Bond experience and *The Monkees* were the embodiment of Richard Lester's Beatles experience. Since *Week* was also based on an English show they thought we understood that style of humor."[8]

According to Gardner, concocting the crazy madcap world of *The Monkees* took a true collaboration between writers, directors, actors and editors. For the writers, generating *The Monkees'* brand of comedy required a return to the solid structure of classic films. "Many of the most successful ideas are about rejiggering existing ideas. We had to generate 32 stories that first season so you go to the classics and there are only X number of classic stories: Charlie's Aunt [became Micky in drag in "The Chaperone"], Romeo and Juliet [became Davy's shotgun near-wedding in "Hillbilly Honeymoon"], identity copies à la *A Tale of Two Cities* [became Micky as a gangster in "Alias Micky Dolenz"]... Then we tried to create an unpleasant authority figure to give the boys a funny way to clash with authority and to attract a good name guest star."[9] Gardner's comments illustrate his understanding of the requirements of writing a thirty-minute situation comedy and what stock types of characters and conflicts needed to be recreated on a weekly basis.

In terms of subversive, counterculture content Gardner did not consider himself part of that movement. In his early thirties, intimately associated with the Kennedy assassination, Gardner had grown up in the last decade and, had what he defined as grown-up obligations. "I was trying to make a living, pay the kids' tuition and orthodontia." To illustrate his immense lack of understanding of the impending counterculture, Gardner tells the story about the time he went to the set as they were filming a typical teenage party at the Monkees' pad. "I wanted to call for the costumer because none of the party guests was wearing a dinner jacket, but the AD [assistant director] said that's not how kids dress for parties anymore so I let it go."[10] The lesson did not take, as in one of Gardner and Caruso's other scripts Peter mentions loaning Davy his new sports coat.

The only non–New Yorker on the staff, Dave Evans, earned the second most credits (nine of 58). He hailed from Kansas and used that as a way to show off his comedic abilities to the producers during his job interview. When Schneider asked where he was from, Evans told the truth, "Hutchinson, Kansas," a small city of several thousand. Then Schneider asked what Hutchinson was near and rather than pick a large city that anyone would be expected to know such as Topeka or Wichita, Evans chose Nickerson, Kansas, population 1,207. Evans felt that the laugh created by that line sealed his contract with Schneider. Evans had moved to Los Angeles after working as a writer of greeting cards and found work on a pilot with Jay Ward of *Bullwinkle* fame. "The show we worked on didn't sell but I found an agent through it—an old, ready to retire one." Then Ward told Evans, "I just saw a pilot for a show that's going to be on in the fall. It's the dumbest thing I've ever seen but you'd be perfect for it." Evans pitched an idea to Associate Producer Ward Sylvester and asked, "Is that what you're looking for?" Sylvester said, "That's exactly what I'm looking for" and Evans was hired. "Of course, the episode I pitched was too expensive for production so it was never made, but Ward hired me because he said it had 'the right spirit' for the show." Evans wrote the first episode to film ("Don't Look a Gift Horse in the Mouth") and co-wrote (with Dolenz) the last to air ("Frodis Caper") so in Evans' words, "I saw the beginning and the end. It was joyful. People really caught that. That's why the audience responded so well."[11]

Apropos to the show, Evans approached writing comedy a bit differently. "Some of the other writers came up with stock locations and situations first and created a bunch of jokes around that—circus, haunted house, etc. I wrote stories first and then found what was funny in the story. *The Monkees* was a loose enough show to accommodate all these different styles and the boys were there to give the audience their continuity." Evans was also one of the few writers to spend any time on the set from the very first episode, "Gift Horse." He remembers, "Bob [Rafelson] [now directing] invited me and my wife to the local farm which served as the set and he kept asking for new jokes here and there all day so I kept rewriting as we filmed. After that collaboration he had me do a lot of writing of what we called the romps, the physical gag stuff the boys would do during song montages."

Evans enjoyed co-writing "Frodis Caper" with Dolenz even though it involved writing in a rush. "Micky always wanted to direct and write so he went to Ward with a story idea and Ward said he could have any of the writers he wanted to work with and he thankfully chose me." They had trouble finalizing the deal since it was an actor requesting a contract as writer and director so Evans and Dolenz had only a day or so to actually write the script. "I went out to Micky's house in Lookout Canyon in a rain storm lugging my typewriter and found him playing clarinet with a house full of other music people jamming. His house was always packed. So I sat down and we wrote it in the midst of that crowd."

Evans enjoyed working on the show immensely but, "The producers valued me because they knew I was right for the show and the show was right for me. But it ruined me for a career in television." He recalled the story of one of *The Monkees* secretaries coming into his office saying, "You're laughing but you're all alone in here." His answer: "I'm a comedy writer. If it doesn't make me laugh I'd better not hand it in." Shortly after the cancelation of *The Monkees* Evans found himself in another office on another show reading his work and thinking, "This doesn't seem funny to me. Uh-oh. This isn't my show and this isn't my business." Evans left the newer show and later considered reviving *The Monkees* with Dolenz in animation à la *Scooby Doo*. "Since animation is what I loved and in animation you could take the characters to the moon or anywhere," but purchasing the rights to the name of the show from the studio was financially prohibitive. Instead, Evans left show business altogether, did industrial and business films that won awards and then chose to follow his family's life of faith. His father had been a Presbyterian minister, so for Evans studying conflict resolution and mediation with a multi-ethnic collection of pastors and priests seemed a natural next step in life. "I wasn't sure it was my calling until I handled my first four mediations, on which I thought I was lousy. But then I did the fifth one and it all clicked and I knew this was the work I was meant to do." He also realized "Comedy provided the essential piece to this new work." Though he did not consider himself a member of the counterculture, Evans' spiritual background meshed well with the ideology of peace and love that the actors began to bring to the program, especially in the second season.

Clearly, neither Gardner nor Evans felt connected to the counterculture. Neither did freelancer Coslough Johnson. To Johnson, "Counterculture meant you were a communist. I was older than the actors and most of the writers since I'd been in the military and then done industrial films so I didn't even know the smell of marijuana. When you walked into the producer's offices on *The Monkees* you smelled that sweet smell. I assumed it was sweet tea." Bernie Orentein added, "My wife accuses me of missing the sixties entirely, and I'm afraid she's right. I avoided the 'emerging counterculture scene' mostly because I didn't know there was one going on. When I worked on *The Monkees*, I was 35 years old, and my 'regular' job was as a writer (including musical-special material) for *The Hollywood Palace* ... a show noted more for Sinatra and Crosby appearances than for the emerging music of the sixties."[12]

At this point it might be easy to assume the injection of counterculture comments in the scripts shows that a large proportion of authorship could be credited to the young actors. A reading of the contributions of writer Peter Meyerson (8 of 58) dispels that thought. Meyerson wrote both the first episode to air ("Royal Flush") and the one that included Frank

Zappa dressed as Mike Nesmith and Mike Nesmith dressed as Frank Zappa ("Monkees Blow Their Minds"). Meyerson, like Gardner, came from New York, "From The Bronx, right near Yankee Stadium when they still owned the Dodgers." He earned a graduate degree in American Literature and taught for a semester at the University of Connecticut only to be offered a job in publishing that paid much better. A television producer he met suggested he write some spec sketches for some of the comedy shows of the era, which Meyerson did. Soon he was writing and producing for WBAI Pacifica Radio with Robert Schlitt, who would become his writing partner on *The Monkees*.[13]

When they were given the offer to come to California for *The Monkees* "we figured we'd take the risk." Soon Meyerson became friendly with the actors, attending parties at Tork's house and happily catching on to the current "scene" which included a party where Tork taught Meyerson's son, Jason, to swim and a different kind of party on another night when, "the most beautiful girl in the world stripped naked and dove into the pool." Soon his scripts were studded with sly ad-libs to the camera that commented on current icons as well as controversies. In "Monkees in a Ghost Town" a call for help is answered first by an Indian who claims "Me cannot help—Me primitive Indian chief. Know nothing about white man's problems." This sly comment on the rising of activity in the Red Power Movement of Indians aired in 1966, three years before Indians would retake and occupy Alcatraz Island off the coast of San Francisco. Later in the episode Meyerson mixes a metatextual moment with a comment on the counterculture when a western deputy answers the second call. This time when Davy says the boys are in trouble the deputy says, "I better get Mr. Dillon." Davy asks, "Marshal Dillon?" referencing the long-running *Gunsmoke*. But the deputy answers, "No, Bob Dylan. He can write a song about your problems." Meyerson was also behind the Vietnam War reference in the domino-playing scene in "Monkee Mother."

After *The Monkees*, Schlitt moved into writing for one-hour dramas including *The Mod Squad, Kung Fu* and *Lou Grant*. Meyerson stuck to comedy, developed *Welcome Back, Kotter* and produced forty-four episodes of the series, which centered around four teenage boys connected by comic delinquency rather than music. To wrap up his time on *The Monkees* Meyerson wrote his last three scripts solo, with some side help from his new colleague, the only female writer on the show, Treva Silverman. Meyerson remembered, "We used to crack each other up. We would just roll around on the floor and laugh. We had a good working relationship, much more productive, creative and fun working relationship with Treva than I ever did with any other partner." Another sign that Meyerson belonged more to the sixties than some of his counterparts comes from the fact that he had no problem working with a female comedy writer as an equal. "It's about who's funniest."

That philosophy must have been shared by the producers who hired Silverman (six of 58 episodes) after a series of meetings in New York. In interviews about the show Silverman often remembers, "We were told that the show was looking for the New York head—the quick wit of the New York personality. They didn't even want a resume. The producers had told the agents they didn't want 'the same old trite Hollywood formula' which, to me, was very exciting. First they held a meeting in a screening room with tons of dark bearded, long-haired guys—and me the only woman asked to be there." Next the producers requested material. Silverman had written sketches for *The Entertainers* (a one-season sketch comedy starring Carol Burnett, Bob Newhart and Dom DeLuise) and her material made the second and third meetings with Ward Sylvester, associate producer and manager of Davy Jones. "On the third meeting I cheekily said, 'So how many more of these meetings do you have in mind?' And happily that's when they said, 'This is the last one. It's to tell you that you're on staff.'" Silverman joined a boys club, mostly from New York, who moved to the West Coast to work on the show.

It's no surprise that Meyerson and Silverman became good friends during their two seasons on the show, to the point where they partnered up for some later work on other series (*Captain Nice, Accidental Family*) because Silverman was the other writer who happily identified with the counterculture world of the time. "I remember going back East and telling my old college roommates that I had started smoking grass. They were shocked. Pot hadn't quite reached the East Coast to the extent that it had invaded the West Coast." Silverman felt deeply that, "I was born a few years too early. I loved everything that was going on. It felt like we'd finally found the key and this was how it's always going to be." She remembers that when they first came to California, Meyerson nailed it. "He realized that New York was vertical and California was horizontal. Here you could spread out and grow and change."[14]

At first Silverman disliked the romps. "I remember referring to them as things that will be interrupting all our wonderful comedy." Regarding authorship and improvisation, she recalled that the writers were requested to write out the entire romp in their first and second scripts and found, "It was a lovely feeling to write the romp." After those early, more detailed romps, the writers were asked only to indicate props and sets and specify a few bits and let the actors and the director improvise the rest. On a deeper issue of authorship, that of inventing character, Silverman remembers all the detailed planning that went into creating the lead characters at early staff meetings after having watched the actors' auditions and the pilot. "That's when I really wanted to be on the show. They were so smart and cute and sweet." They decided Mike would represent "us," the leader, the one with his feet on the ground; Micky was meant to be the crazy off-the-wall type; Davy was a heartthrob, and then they came to the decision whether Peter would play a genius or a total idiot. "It was like voting on deciding the Pope. Sadly Peter was so smart and so perceptive and so insightful and yet we decided to make his character a total idiot for the sake of the comedy."[15]

Yet Silverman understands the audience's confusion over authorship on television in general and *The Monkees* in particular. She shared the memory of a conversation with her mother who often called and was told her daughter was in a story meeting. "But after watching the show my mother asked if they were telling the truth, 'There are no stories on *The Monkees,*'" a comment contrary to the earlier assertions of Gardner and Dolenz. Silverman's youthful enthusiasm for the work informed the episodes she wrote, including "I've Got a Little Song Here," where a naïve Mike tries to sell a song to a major pop star, and "One Man Shy," where Peter woos a woman out of his league. In her own life her excitement about making a career of writing is contagious, especially when recalling her favorite memory of working on *The Monkees*. "I always liked writing at night. When everyone would leave at 6 or 6:30 I would start and I would write late into the night. I remember distinctly late one night walking across the studio lot, the lights coming down, the only thing I could hear was the sound of my own shoes clicking on the cement and I very distinctly thought, 'This is Hollywood. This is writing. This is it.'" For Silverman it was the start of a comedy-writing career that would encompass winning two Best Writing Emmys in 1974. One came for Best Writing in comedy for *The Mary Tyler Moore Show* episode "The Lou and Edie Story" where Edie Grant asks Lou Grant for a divorce. The other was as Writer of the Year—Series.

During their many reunion concerts across the years the members of *The Monkees* have frequently credited the songwriters for the longevity of the music. Certainly Neil Diamond, Carole King, Gerry Goffin and Carole Bayer Sager and the other songwriters proved their worth as songwriters. But so did this stellar staff of comedy writers prove their worth in the medium of their choice. From *The Monkees* they went on to write, create, produce and earn Emmys on such '70s staples as *Laugh-In, The Mary Tyler Moore Show, Sanford and Son, Welcome Back, Kotter, Laverne and Shirley* and contribute to comedy films including *Big* and *Romancing the Stone*. These writers deserve to be remembered for how their timeless comedy has kept the show alive across the generations and so contributed equally to the ongoing success of *The Monkees*.

Four

The Kind of Girl I Could Love

Feminism, Gender and Sexuality

In a world attuned to reruns of *Two and a Half Men* and *The Big Bang Theory*, where beloved male characters spend the bulk of their time skirt-chasing and notching (or dreaming of notching) their bedposts, it is remarkable that a program about four teenage rock and roll musicians in the free love fallout of the 1960s provided lessons in feminism to their fans. These lessons did not come easily to the show, its writers, creators and network executives but *The Monkees'* balancing act between modernity and traditionaism in its discourse exhibited realistic tensions between feminist ideology and the normative behavior and ideology toward women of an earlier era.

In 58 episodes none of the fictional Monkees ever ended up in bed with a woman, they never mistreated a woman and almost never chased the skirt of a bimbo. Only once did a lead character make a sexually provocative joke. In "Success Story" the three others pretend to be Davy's staff. While quizzing them all on their servile roles, Davy asks Micky, "As my chauffeur how would you help a young lady into the backseat of my car?" Using his snide accent, Micky answers, "As quickly as possible." Being such a rare digression it most likely illustrates a comedy writer's rush for a joke, at the expense of a character since skirt-chaser never defined any of the characters, especially not Micky. Also, in a nod to age diversity, actress Rose Marie appeared twice as a guest star on the show, bringing the Sally Rogers seal of approval to the *The Monkees* while each time portraying a financially independent, middle-aged woman.[1] In the previously discussed "Monkee Mother" Marie portrays an independent widow and in "Monkees in a Ghost Town" she's the Big Woman, leader of a gang of criminals, rather than merely a gangster's moll. Likewise, Elisabeth Fraser (better known to television audiences as Sgt. Bilko's long-suffering girlfriend, Sgt. Joan Hogan in *The Phil Silvers Show*) portrayed a female judge, a rarity on most one-hour dramas of the day, in "The Picture Frame."

The majority of women on the program were in the age range of the lead characters so it is noticeable that the various young women the characters of Davy, Micky, Mike and Peter fall in love with are almost all feminists, defined by their interest in academia, their working for wages and the fact that they are active, not passive, in the various storylines in which they appear. Most of the female characters appearing on the program were self-motivated, mature and responsible. Many held non-gendered careers such as Russian spies, biker chicks and musicians from an all-woman rock band. From academically advanced Vanessa (in the pilot), to Valerie the debutante (in "One Man Shy"), to April Conquest, the laundromat employee (in "Monkees Get Out More Dirt") each young woman has a goal in life which she actively pursues, a goal not limited to gaining the love of a boy. While the discourse evident in most of *The Monkees* epsiodes may not directly advocate for the social, political, legal and economic rights that feminists of the second wave were demanding in the late 1960s, the mere presence of such solid role models deserves discussion. The Monkees most often interact with and fall for young women with careers and always "nice girls," never druggies or drop-outs. The lesson became if women wanted to marry a Monkee, a common dream for the huge female fan base, they should strive to be feminists, not floozies. For many, that lesson lasted most of their lives with former Monkees' fans becoming everything from Ph.D.s to fashion designers (Stella McCartney[2]) to politial commentators (Rachel Maddow). The exposure to such proactive role models may have played a part in fueling those zealous female fans who took to the streets with "Hands off Davy" banners begging the U.S. Army not to draft Davy Jones to fight in the Vietnam War.[3]

In 1960s television the rules of what single characters could and could not do were more stringent. Viewers always saw Ann Marie, on *That Girl,* shut the front door on her boyfriend Donald as he left after a date, rather than shutting the bedroom door on the audience. In 1969 Robert and Carol Brady would be the first married couple to be seen sharing a bed together. So perhaps if sexual activity did not appear on a television landscape, *The Monkees'* writers do not deserve credit for avoiding rampant sexual activity. The FCC would not allow such behavior. But the writers still could have created two-dimensional, unsubstantial females for the characters to date. Instead, the writers created independent female characters to interact with the young male leads of the show. Treva Silverman, one of the first female writers to work solo on a comedy staff partially accounts for the strong female voice on the show. Her presence on the writing staff is an example of the gains women made in the wake of the second wave of feminism, represented in the world of *The Monkees* via its female guest characters. However, coming so early in the second wave of feminism these female guest characters exhibited polysemic behavior in regards to their own feminist discourse. This provides the tension between traditionalism and modernity, with modernity eventually taking the lead.

While the first wave of feminism is generally accepted as beginning with the Seneca Falls Convention in 1848 and ending with the passage of the Nineteenth Amendment in August 1920, feminist scholars argue over the exact beginning of second wave feminism. Was it 1963 with the publication of *The Feminine Mytique* by Betty Freidan or was it 1966 with Friedan's founding of NOW (National Organization of Women)? Was it 1967 when Senator Eugene McCarthy introduced the Equal Rights Amendment in the United States Senate or 1968 when Robin Morgan lead radical feminists on a protest against the Miss America pageant? (*The Monkees* gently mocked the pageant in 1966 when Micky slid down the spiral staircase banister to Mike's singing "There she is, Miss America" in "Royal Flush.") Whatever the moment, those dates occur before and during the run of *The Monkees* and clearly affected the kinds of women, young and old, showcased on the program. First wave feminists fought for opportunity and political empowerment. From the Civil War through World War I they put their campaigns on hold to help with each successive war effort, a sacrifice that kept moving the achievement of their goal of gaining the vote further and further away. For a time, they even considered a rider on their proposed amendment that would only grant the vote to white women. Finally, they attained the support of Congress to ratify the Nineteenth Amendment without the rider in 1920.

Second wavers, arriving in the context of the anti-war civil rights movements of the 1960s, fought for social and educational equality and equal rights in the boardroom and the bedroom. The third wave emerged in the 1990s, characterized by the understanding that not all women want the same things, but all women want and deserve choice in the things they want. Seeds of these desires can be found in some episodes of *The Monkees*. Yet while the female guest characters on *The Monkees* became second wave role models for the viewing audience, the polysemy comes from the fact that they sometimes seemed to sabotage their new message while alternately showing a hint of what was to come in the third wave feminism of the 1990s. Somehow the female guest characters of *The Monkees* maintained their sexuality while obtaining their equal status among the men, living the feminist writer Pinkfloor's quote "It's possible to have a push up bra and a brain at the same time."[4] With a slight fashion change, these second wave women were proving it was possible to have a bikini and a brain at the same time.

Feminists wearing bikinis began showing up in *The Monkees* in the Paul Mazursky and Larry Tucker-penned pilot "Here Come the Monkees" with three females of interest: Davy's first love interest, the soon-to-be-sweet-sixteen Vanessa Russell (Robyn Millan); their manager's assistant, Jill Gunther (Jill Van Ness); and Vanessa's mother (June Whitley Taylor). On the eve of her sixteenth birthday party, to be held at her father's elite country club, the father and daughter audition bands to play the event. Mr. Russell wants something more sedate and traditional. Vanessa wants the Monkees. Though her father will be paying the bill it is Vanessa who persuades him to go with her unorthodox choice. When Vanessa's interest in Davy keeps her out late the night before her history final, her mother advises, "Haven't you been spending too much time with that boy? When you should have been studying." Only 42 percent of female high school graduates attended college in 1966.[5] Vanessa's mother exhibits feminist ideology in prioritizing education over husband-seeking, which would require the opposite—spending more time with a boy than with her studies. When Davy and his bandmates learn that Vanessa failed the final, their reaction goes against the norm as well. Rather than offer her a discourse on how lame school is, which might be expected since none of these long-haired musicians are in college, the Monkees work hard to help Vanessa pass her make-up exam, which she does. Grades are important to Vanessa and helping his girlfriend achieve her educational goals is important to Davy and his fellow bandmates. Though an argument could be made for the fact that she needed the help of male friends to pass her final, the episode makes it clear she could have done so by herself if she had not spent so much time with Davy. Beyond the Russell family, it is Jill the manager's assistant who proactively alerts the Monkees to Vanessa's problem. Then she defends them in front of her boss by saying, "The boys are only trying to help Vanessa pass her final" when he demands to know where Vanessa has gone that day. By premiering their show with a female guest character in the 1960s who cares about her education, *The Monkees* writers have, as Vanessa says to Davy regarding their relationship, "started a trend." A trend that continues across all 58 episodes.

While the pilot, "Here Come the Monkees," was filmed first, it did not air first. The Emmy-winning episode that premiered the show, "Royal Flush," displays similar feminist ideology through the character of Princess Bettina of the Duchy of Harmonica (Katherine Walsh). In DVD commentary provided by Jones in 2003 he remarks that staff writers Peter Meyerson and Robert Schlitt created one of the best written episodes. The story centers around Davy saving the princess from drowning only to learn that her domineering guardian, Uncle Otto, intends for her to die before her 18th birthday, before she can become queen which will render him powerless. Unlike the geeky, awkward teenager in the Meg Cabot book series *The Princess Diaries* (2000) and the films of the same name, the 17-year-old Princess Bettina is mature, intelligent, responsible and modest. She first appears in a one-piece swimsuit, rather than a bikini, and in her later conversation with Davy she discusses her many responsibilites regarding "the welfare of all my people." In an example of the show's ability to make the long-haired Monkees into heroes, it is Davy who urges her to do her duty, rather than run off with him to his beach house. In a riff on *Roman Holiday* (1953), he reminds her, "You're the queen, that's what you have to do." Meanwhile, being an honorable royal, she refuses to believe that her uncle is capable of murder and is only convinced by Davy's audio recording of Otto revealing his plan. The episode then flips the taking-the-female-hostage trope. In order to force Princess Bettina to cooperate with him, Otto's bodyguard holds the Monkees hostage, leaving young male lives in the hands of a young female. As will become a usual plot point of the program, the day is saved through the teamwork of all four boys, but throughout the story Bettina has actively participated in her own salvation. Granted, the audience first met her in a swimsuit and not a business suit, so some old order sexism existed, but her personality overcame that and presented a feminist role model to young female viewers. Finally, in the end-of-show cast interview an interesting gender-bending moment occurs. When asked what they are doing that night Micky says he is looking at next week's script to try to save it, but Davy says he wants to go home to set his hair. This was certainly not the answer America expected from a male romantic lead actor. This episode impressed not only fans, but professional peers as it was nominated for and won James Frawley the Emmy for Outstanding Directorial Achievement in a Comedy Series for the 1966/67 Television season.

It was Peter's turn for a love interest in "One Man Shy" and his choice is also a woman of position and power, debutante Valerie Cartwright (Lisa James). At the height of the popularity of *Bonanza*, 'Cartwright' is a code word for rich, strong, and independent. This first season episode opens on the band yet again auditioning to play a party with the properly themed song "You Just May Be the One." While Valerie enjoys the music, it is clear from her camera POV that she finds Peter the most attractive of the group. She hires them for the party despite the fact that her elitist boyfriend, Ronnie Farnsworth (George Furth), dislikes them intensely. When the lovesick Peter bumps into Ronnie on the way out, Ronnie snaps, "A gentleman does not stare at a lady," to which Peter responds dreamily, "A beggar can look at a queen." Back at the Monkees' pad viewers find that Peter has purloined a portrait of Valerie. He moons over it to the point that his bandmates offer to teach him to talk to such a high class woman. Valerie and Ronnie arrive unexpectedly, discover the painting, and rather than call the authorities, as Ronnie intends, Valerie overrides him and tells Peter he can return the portrait at the party. When Ronnie tries to show her the Monkees are too low class to associate with her by besting them at skeet shooting, archery and badminton, she supports them and turns on Ronnie: "In shaming those boys you humiliated me and yourself." In retaliation she invites Peter to be her escort at the party. There the others attempt to make Peter a member of the upper class by masquerading as his stock broker (Micky), private English tailor (Davy), and yacht captain (Mike). When Ronnie exposes them as frauds Valerie dismisses his action and tells Peter, "I think you're a fine enough person just being yourself." A charming comedic moment occurs earlier in the episode when the boys try to help Peter win a game of Spin the Bottle with an uncredited guest actress only to learn that the bottle always points to Davy even when he has left the room. The guest actress is also portrayed as a friend, trying to help Peter overcome his insecurity with women, and not merely a sex object.

Feminist ideology could not be any more prominent than the opening line of "I Was a 99 lb. Weakling" when Micky tells his current girlfriend Brenda, "You know, physical beauty isn't enough. I guess that's why I fell in love with you, Brenda. I wanted a girl with some intelligence." Instead of choosing Micky, who refers to her by her given name, the bikini-clad Brenda traditionally chooses a buff beach bruiser (David Draper) who refers to her generically as a chick. Feeling skinny and scrawny, Micky attempts to build up his muscles to win her back. He has to hock his drums to pay for an expensive health guru, which Davy notes will break up the group. When Peter asks Micky if she is worth it, he answers, "She's beautiful and brilliant and intelligent." Note that two of the three adjectives have to do with her intellect and only one with her looks. Never is a woman of value on the program if she is only beautiful. As the episode continues, to save the drums his band mates spend the rest of the episode helping Micky buff up. When he's back on the beach with Brenda in the finale, a cliché nerd with thick, black glasses nearly trips over their blanket while walking and reading Proust. Brenda immediately attaches herself to the reader by saying, "Oh, I just love a man with a mind," leaving Micky muttering, "She wants his mind. I have a mind." While Brenda was not one of the nicer young female characters created by the writers and seemed to sink into traditionalism when she kept choosing the stronger man, in the end she exhibited a more modern feminist ideology in her desire for a mate of matching intelligence.

It is interesting to note that the writers never created an episode around a love interest for Mike's character, possibly because the audience knew from reading popular magazines that Nesmith was the only married actor in *The Monkees*. It was standard practice in this era not to make married actors into ladies men when possible. Producers felt the audience did not want to feel guilty when watching their favorite stars. Therefore the producers of *The Monkees* may have thought it would be wrong to portray the Mike character as chasing after other women. Or it could be his air of maturity, which lead to his position as the leader and father figure of the band, kept Mike from capturing the mood of a mooning teenager. However, in "Monkees Get Out More Dirt" (Gerald Gardner and Dee Caruso) all four band members find themselves falling in love with the same woman, April Conquest (Julie Newmar). April runs the local laundromat and is also pursuing a postgraduate degree, albeit a farsical master's degree in laundry science. Yet pursuing a master's implies she already has a bachelor's degree in an era where few women finished their bachelors, much less started them. Again, a Monkee (or in this case all four) are portrayed as finding intellectual women appealing. This polysemic predicament presents a character that is motivated and educated, but only inside the parameters of the non-threatening, stereotypically feminine world of laundry. Therefore April's character is both resisting and conforming to gendered stereotypes. The episode also features a female expert, Dr. Lorene Sisters (Claire Kelley), as host of an advice for the lovelorn program in the style of the real life Dr. Joyce Brothers, whose name the writers gently mock. This plot allows the writers, Gerald Gardener and Dee Caruso, to delve into how modern men should court modern women by learning what hobbies interest these modern women. Dr. Sisters openly states, "The fastest way to a woman's heart, is through her mind," acknowledging a man's romantic job is to "find out what kind of a man she likes, and then be that man." Each Monkee researches what April likes and returns to the laundromat to woo her: Davy by painting a pop art mural, Peter by playing chamber music on a piano, Micky by dancing ballet and Mike by riding a motorcycle. Of the four hobbies, all but motorcycle riding are high class concerns, making April both an educated and cultured female. Soon Davy's query, "I wonder what it would be like going through life with a girl like that" leads the viewer into the weekly music romp where their various futures with April are imagined to the tune of Micky singing "The Girl I Knew Somewhere." This manner of marriage—or "going through life with a girl like that"—seems to be fine until jealousy breaks up the band—and their friendship. Portioning out of the pad into four sections (leaving Peter the TV, Micky the empty icebox, Davy the front door and Mike the bathroom) provides visual proof of the destruction of their friendship. Further, the confusion over being attracted to four men at the same time threatens April's health. For her sake (rather than their own happiness) the Monkees agree to draw straws. Peter wins and Micky, Mike and Davy break up with April while extolling Peter's qualities. In the necessary comedic twist, April leaves Peter for a singer, the very talent all four Monkees mastered before she entered their lives. Again, while the illness caused by April having to choose between the four Monkees could be evidence of stereotypical feminine delicacy, her work ethic, goals and cultured interests speak to the second wave feminism ideology represented in the episode. What April wanted in a man was much more than women before her had been allowed to want. As a true second wave feminist, April wanted both professional and personal satisfaction. The tensions between modernity and traditionalism made her ill.

The overall feminist discourse nurtured by the creative team on the show continued in the second season. "Wild Monkees" offers a look at both feminism and masculinity with a side order of gender-bending when a pack of female bikers arrives at a broken down old hotel where the band is playing, while also working as bell hops and waiters to earn the right to play. Upon their arrival, swathed in sunglasses, helmets and scarves, the female bikers are assumed to be men until one of them kisses Davy, revealing herself to be a female to the audience and to Davy. The leader, Queenie, and her crew of biker chicks are physically stronger than the Monkees, which does not keep the Monkees from wanting to woo them. Certainly, some comedy is gained from playing on the lead males' weakness when compared to strength and aggression of the biker women. Yet the overriding sense is that the men are still attracted to tough women, a new thought in the sixties. Their strength makes the young women more appealing, yet the musicians' lack of strength still attracts the women who call Micky "Fuzzy," tell Peter he's a sissy for quoting poetry and tell Mike he makes too many 'funny faces' and resembles a cocker spaniel. In the face of this rejection, the boys decide they have to, in Micky's words, "find a way to get really, really rough," contradicting Dr. Sisters' adivce in "Monkees Get Out More Dirt." They form a biker group of their own and pledge to "obey the laws of dirt and violence," "curb their desire for a bath" and "offend all living things." They believe these rules will make them more appealing to Queenie.[6] However, she and the other biker women now find the Monkees 'too tough' and say they left their boyfriends, the Black Angels Biker Gang, for that very reason. When the male bikers, the Black Angels, arrive on the scene and challenge the Monkees to a fight, the Monkees immediately rename their club The Chickens to avoid trouble. Queenie's boyfriend, Butch, threatens to beat up any or all of them just for fun and she refuses to allow him to hurt any of them. In response to her aggressive attitude, Butch shouts at her to shut up. At this moment, the feminist ideology wavers and, rather than yell back in the face of his disrespect, Queenie sweetly insists she missed Butch, apparently for his gruffness. Before the episode can further diffuse the feminist stance it took, the Black Angels challenge the Monkees to a motorcycle race. After the Monkees win, Butch begins to assault Micky. Queenie proactively threatens: "You touch one hair on his head and I'll never let you write to me!" This time Butch relents. Further, when Queenie tells Butch: "I'm tired of the open road. I'm tired of the dust and the grime and the bugs in my teeth. I want to settle down. We could build illegal motorcycles and raise little scooters" Butch makes the feminist statement: "My woman speaks for me" and seems to insist all the gang members will follow his lead and listen to their women's needs and wants. While the overall ending, women choosing to settle down rather than ride off into the sunset on adventures, seems at first to be a statement against the goals of the second wave feminists, it is in fact an early statement of third wave feminism: there is nothing wrong with having a home and family as long as that is your own choice. Choice has always been a major plank of any wave of feminism from the first wavers protesting for the right to choose political leaders through access to the voting booth, to the second wavers protesting for the right to choose contraception and family planning, to the third wavers protesting for the right to choose their own multiple definitions of feminism and success.[7]

Another blend of feminist perspectives appears in the all-girl rock group the Monkees encounter in "Some Like It Lukewarm" as both groups compete for a $500 first prize at a TV talent show. The contest is only open to co-ed groups which requires Davy to grudgingly dress as a female. The contest manager, Jerry, falls for Davy's impression of a female and follows him home, requiring Davy to stay in disguise until the group's second performance the next night. In training Davy to be a woman, Peter quotes three lessons from the fictional etiquette book, "How to Act Like a Feminine Female in 3 Easy Lessons." Each lesson is impossible for Davy, or any actual woman, to master and enacting this charade shows how outdated these descriptions of femininity are to an audience in the late 1960s. At the contest The Monkees tie with The West Minstrel Abbies, whose male lead singer is actually Daphne (played by Deana Martin), a female guitarist disguised as a male. Davy describes "him" as "a bit effeminate," an oddly ironic comment for Davy to make while wearing a wig. Noticeable in this episode is the fact that the other Monkees tend to condescend to Davy when he is dressed as a female, showing anti-feminist sentiments not normal for their characters when interacting with real females. The other anti-feminist moment in the episode comes once the secret is out about both groups having a member dressed in drag. Rather than lose the chance to win the contest, they combine into one co-ed group that wins the contest. There the women, who formerly played their own guitars, become nothing more than mini-skirted, go-go girls, dancing and singing backup to the boys, though previously they had held their own on stage, winning equal audience applause. Apparently 1967 was too early to imagine the future success of Ann and Nancy Wilson of Heart or Amy Ray and Emily Saliers of the Indigo Girls. Still the episode offers more pro-feminist messages than con. When Davy and Daphne realize the fraud they are both playing, Daphne asks why Davy didn't divulge his true identity, at least to her. Davy replies, "I didn't think that a girl as nice and considerate and as pretty as you would go for somebody who wasn't honest." Again, the things that attract a Monkee to a potential date are not first looks, but rather quality of character.

Finally, among female role models, Rose Marie represented second wave feminism filtering into the middle-aged generation, the one born between first and second waves. Forty-two when she guest starred on the series, Marie came to the show with the reputation of having played Sally Rogers, the only female on the writing staff populated by the other characters on *The Dick Van Dyke Show* (1961–1966). For "Monkees in a Ghost Town" (written by Meyerson and Schlitt) Marie plays Bessie Kowalsky, arriving halfway through an episode where two cliché gangsters named Lenny and George have thrown the Monkees into the Old West-style jail, awaiting the arrival of the Big Man. Instead, Bessie enters demanding "the loot" only to be dismissed by George and told that the PTA meeting is down the block. She doesn't suffer fools gladly, insisting she's not the welcome wagon, another female-centric group, either. "I'm the Big Woman. The Big Man's wife," but "He got too big. Now I'm the Big Man." When George thinks she is lying and must be The Monkees' mother, here to rescue them, she gives him a karate flip to show her strength. The Monkees cheer her on, until she tells Lenny to "take 'em out and shoot 'em" so as not to leave any witnesses, showing no trace of traditional maternal mercy. Instead of appealing to her maternal nature, the Monkees appeal to her former life as an entertainer and ask to perform one more number, with her, during which time George and Lenny join them onstage, trading their gun for Davy's maracas. An old-fashioned, western shoot-out occurs in the saloon, which the Monkees finally win. In the tag, as the policemen handcuff Bessie, she says that while in jail she, George and Lenny are going to work up a new act called Bessie and the Bullets. Even in jail she will be the leader of their group.

In Rose Marie's second episode as Milly Rudnick in "Monkee Mother" (written by Meyerson and Schlitt) the episode's ending illustrates marriage as a vehicle for her true happiness, similar to the message ending "Wild Monkees," but this idea plays out more as an easy way of giving the Monkees back the independence of their living arrangement and not as a statement that marriage was a woman's ultimate goal. Milly moves in when the boys can't pay their rent and allows them to stay on as boarders. She treats them as a mother, making them do chores and playing matchmaker for Davy. From the start she declares, "You can call me Milly, but that doesn't mean you can step all over me." Actually, Milly proceeds to order them around, asking them to help the moving man carry in all her furniture, clean the house, fix the car, fix the plumbing and wash the dishes. In the musical romp to "Sometime in the Morning" there is a fantasy sequence where Milly imagines herself 17 again, dancing with each of the Monkees individually, all dressed in period costumes rather than modern day clothing. Throughout the episode Milly gives each boy the positive support of a nurturing mother, but her smothering ways are hard for the Monkees to adapt to and soon Micky is caught feeding Peter by flying the spoon around him to the sound of airplane engines. Mike says, "There isn't any way out—we might as well be married to her." Micky builds on the idea, "We'll find her a husband. That's what she needs. That's what she wants." Noticeably, he corrects himself, moving from the cliché "needs" to the feminist "wants," and the band goes about making sure Milly gets what she *wants* by setting her up with the moving man. The two eventually marry and The Monkees play "Look Out, Here Comes Tomorrow" at the reception held conveniently in their no-longer-to-be-shared apartment.

Though some of these episodes seem to falter in their feminist discourse and agenda, a few of them actually pass the Bechdel Test, created in 1985 by comic artist Alison Bechdel in her comic strip *Dykes to Watch Out For*. There she laid out a character's criteria for the existence of feminism in a film (later applied to television and other media). To pass the Bechdel Test the story has to involve (1) at least two female characters (2) who talk to each other (3) about something besides a man.[8] By these strict guidelines, a program starring four female leads such as *Sex and the City* often fails as they more often than not only engage in discussions about men, but *The Monkees*, starring four male leads, succeeds. By design many episodes contained young female characters who fell in love with the Monkees and most scenes involving females involved them interacting with the Monkees, but both the pilot and "Some Like It Lukewarm" contain scenes involving two female characters discussing something besides the male leads of the series. In the pilot it is Vanessa and her mother and later Vanessa and her teacher who discuss Vanessa's scores on her history final, and in "Some Like It Lukewarm" the scenes involve the four members of the all-girl band discussing their chances of winning the contest. A scene passing the Bechdel Test also appears in "Monkees à la Mode" (foreshadowing *The Devil Wears Prada*) when fashion magazine editor, Madame Quagmeyer, discusses cover story ideas with female editorial assistant, Toby Willis. Toby recommends feautring the Monkees on the cover as Typical Young Americans, but she is discussing them as subjects in her journalistic career, not as potential romantic interests. In fact, that episode, though including this young female character, is not in the romantic comedy genre but rather an episode centering around the theme of how fame effects people.

Finally, feminist ideology found its way into what seemed the least feminist aspect of the show—the coverage of the individual actors and their wives in the teen press of the day, consumed mainly by teen girls. Fame, and teen magazines, made the wives role models to viewers as well. For example, teen magazines held Phyllis Nesmith up as an "ideal celebrity wife" for her morals and ability to manage motherhood in the midst of her husband's chaotic life.[9] Between the first and second seasons, Dolenz publicly courted and then married Samantha Juste, a young woman with her own career and her own fame as a host of *Top of the Pops*, a British television program featuring popular music. These real world women were living the tensions of the time in a way the young female characters on the program could only attempt to reflect. So in both their fictional world and in what part of their real lives made it into the press, Monkees men were portrayed as wanting independent women of intelligence and substance.

Five

Early Morning Blues and Greens
An Ethnic Studies Look
at Minority Representation

The Monkees' debut on NBC in September of 1966 came just before the organization of several strikes on college campuses such as San Francisco State and the University of California, Berkeley, held to demand the creation of ethnic studies departments which would teach the history of various ethnic groups alongside the predominant, European-centric version. It was not possible to look at *The Monkees* through the prism of ethnic studies during its initial run on television, but it is possible—and is also enlightening—to do so now. *The Monkees'* run on NBC came at the tail end of the Civil Rights Movement that urged the expansion of ethnic studies and in the midst of the Red Power Movement that would culminate in the occupation of Alcatraz Island in 1969. While Asian Americans founded the Asian Coalition for Equality (ACE) in Seattle in this era, the National Italian American Foundation would not be created until 1975, as a response to *The Godfather*, which made Italians more than cliché caricatures with funny accents and a proclivity towards pasta (by turning them into modern day American cowboys or cold-blooded killers, depending on your perspective, but that's another story). Additionally, *The Monkees* arrived before the initials AARP reached peak power and recognition in the mission to guard the rights of or exploit the power of (depending on your politics) the retired and the elderly. Thanks to the growing clout of the Civil Rights Movement, African Americans fared better on the program, while ethnic minorities such as Gypsies, Russians and Indians, but particularly Asians and Italians, suffered from cliché characterizations guaranteed to get a cheap laugh. Yet characters over the age of 65, those one would expect the youth culture to demean the most, were more often shown as three-dimensional people with hopes and dreams quite similar to the hopes and dreams of the lead characters on *The Monkees*.

Deeper study of the representation of each group on *The Monkees* shows that most of these ethnic groups earned cliché representation and though African Americans were never victims of caricature, as guest characters on the program they were still in short supply. An argument could be made that being a mix of both Italian and Native American, Micky Dolenz the actor gave Micky the character permission to engage in more ethnic behavior than an African American character could in 1960s television. At that time, African American characters had been more pristine types, later nicknamed "Oreos": Bill Cosby in *I Spy* (1965–1968), Ivan Dixon on *Hogan's Heroes* (1965–1970), Nichelle Nichols on *Star Trek* (1966–1969). Families that would not watch a program starring an African American, such as *The Sammy Davis Jr. Show* (1966) or *Hawk* (1966), might let their children watch *The Monkees* and therefore accidentally allow the children to experience these new cultures. Ties between the Italian American community and the African American community have existed ever since Sicilians from the South of Italy emigrated to the Southern United States and found themselves working together in the sugar and cotton fields of the Jim Crow South. The darker complexion of the Sicilians classed them as non-white, though not yet as "colored," an odd limbo to be sure.[1] In fact, the largest mass lynching in America did not involve African Americans but Italian immigrants in New Orleans in 1891. There nineteen men were accused of the murder of police lieutenant David Hennessey, found not guilty by a jury, but eleven were dragged from prison and lynched by an angry mob, giving the two cultures a shared fear of race-based discrimination.[2] Finally, the media compounded this conjunction of the two cultures. Often Italian Americans stood in for African American characters in early films, right on up to Disney's animated *The Jungle Book* where Louis Prima performed the voice of King Louie, the orangutan. The film premiered in the middle of the run of *The Monkees*, in 1967, showing media representations often found it natural to equate Italian Americans with African Americans. Both cultures also shared the experience of being often equated with inner-city, low-income, criminal life styles in film and television.

This conjunction continued into the world of rock and roll. While inducting classic blue-eyed soul group The Rascals into the Rock and Roll Hall of Fame, E Street Band guitarist Steven Van Zandt claimed, "To be white and sound that black you've *got* to be Italian."[3] He might also have been speaking of Micky the Monkee who served as both comic foil, as emerging ethnic characters tend to do (think Raj on *The Big Bang Theory*) and had a propensity for singing "black" music ("Goin Down," "I Got a Woman," "Johnny B. Goode") while offering homage to black performers such as James Brown in live concerts. In the liner notes to the band's greatest hits album released in 1995, written by Ken Barnes, Micky's performance of "I'm a Believer" is described as being "imbued with a characteristic testifying gospel flavor." Micky's character (and Dolenz' personal taste in solo songs) likely introduced middle American viewers to performers they might never have known and helped pave the way for the acceptance of *The Flip Wilson Show* (1970), J.J. "Dy-no-mite" Evans (Jimmy Walker) on *Good Times* (1974) and Venus Flytrap (Tim Reid) on *WKRP in Cincinnati* (1978). By allowing the Italian-descended Dolenz to be more ethnic on television, other African American characters could later be allowed to be so as well.

In 1968, fourteen years after Brown vs. Board of Education of Topeka, Kansas, African American representation began to grow away from Jim Crow characters in many forms of media. That year, Charles Schultz refused to take Franklin, his African American character, out of the school setting with the rest of the Peanuts characters as suggested by fans against the Brown vs. Board decision.[4] Tim Reid and Tom Dreesen, billed as the first interracial comedy duo, had a hard time finding clubs where they were allowed to perform together and that allowed desegregated audiences.[5] Yet in that same time frame, Davy Jones took one of the strongest stands for African American equality on the show. He could and did introduce Charlie Smalls, later composer of *The Wiz* (1975), as his current song writing partner in the second season after-episode-interview segment of "Some Like It Lukewarm." A year earlier, Peter had laid the groundwork by discussing invoking the Civil Rights Act of 1964 regarding his civil right to wear his hair long in an after-episode-interview involving the Sunset Strip riots.

Within its fictional universe, and as a comedy, the show could not present stories involving the types of conflicts and protests then being created on college campuses and lunch counters around the country. Since the characters as rock musicians did not even attend college, those stories would have been out of place in many ways. Also, casting directors were still adjusting to the successes of the Civil Rights Movement and did not expressly cast many people of color as extras for party scenes at the Monkees' pad or in other scenes involving crowds. The one time they did cast a preponderance of people of color happened in "The Devil and Peter Tork" where the jury of convicts included two African Americans and three or more darker, possibly Hispanic types amid a few tough-looking rednecks. This is ironic in that by October 1967 Thurgood Marshall had taken his seat as the first African American judge on the Supreme Court.

One therefore reads the attitude of the show's creators toward the Civil Rights Movement in the guest characters of color added to several episodes. In "I've Got a Little Song Here" we find the Monkees have an African American mail carrier named Bobby with whom they share friendly banter and clearly a respectful relationship. Bobby clearly makes more money than the band and they respect him for that. In "Monkees in the Ring" (written by Gardner and Caruso) the character of color is The Champ, an African American champion fighter who speaks in rhymes à la Cassius Clay/Muhammad Ali. Played by D'Urville Martin (a year before his appearance in the film *Guess Who's Coming to Dinner*) the character is talented and confident and even refers to himself as "The Greatest." At first critical glance, the fact that such a lead guest character is not even given a name, only called "The Champ" even in closing credits, could illustrate lack of respect. However, the white fighter who takes a fall for a bribe is also named only "The Smasher" in dialogue and in credits so it was style choice and not a slighting of the minority character. The other time the show referenced Muhammad Ali came quickly in "Your Friendly Neighborhood Kidnappers." As another hood, played by Vic Tayback, attempts to do a modern dance the words "Cassius Clay Watch Out" appear on screen, odd because this episode aired in October of 1966, but Clay had changed his name to Muhammad Ali two years earlier. Perhaps the writers and network executives felt their audience demographic would more easily remember "Clay" by his old name rather than his new one— or perhaps they rejected that early injection of Islam into their Christian-Judeo-dominated culture.

In "A Nice Place to Visit" (written by Treva Silverman) the Monkeemobile breaks down in a small, Mexican town terrorized by El Diablo/The Bandit Without a Heart. They have to go undercover as rival Mexican banditos to help the town break El Diablo's hold. Though the bulk of the guest characters are of Mexican descent, the Monkees encounter an African American character (played by Godfrey Cambridge) demanding a fifty-cent fee for parking the Monkeemobile in his field. When the Monkees question his authenticity, he answers, "If you can be Mexican bandits, I can be a Mexican parking lot attendant." Played for comedy, this moment also speaks to one of the goals of the Civil Rights Movement, that of allowing people of color to enter any profession of their choosing. Comedian and Tony-award nominated Godfrey Cambridge played this brief cameo role. Cambridge had just been included in a list of four of the era's most celebrated comedians of color in the era, alongside Dick Gregory, Bill Cosby and Nipsy Russell.[6] One wonders whether the producers and casting director assumed the teenage audience knew Cambridge and was his casting another nod to counterculture ideas?

Of interest is why no other episode used Mexican American characters, whether as clichéd caricatures or not. It is possible the writers only used this ethnicity once because in the 1960s Mexican American populations still clustered in the West and Southwest, not yet an immigrant experience common to middle Americans in the way Italian and Asian Americans immigrants were. At the time, most Americans' exposure to Mexican Americans came from the media, specifically advertising and more specifically the Frito Bandito of Frito-Lay fame. Even Speedy Gonzales had only been present in Looney Tunes since 1953. Cesar Chavez's larger profile would come in the midst of and after *The Monkees* left the air (late '60s–early '70s) and in its infancy revolved more around the union movement than the Chicano movement. One inclusive moment for Spanish-speaking listeners came in the second season, "The Monkees Christmas Show." Instead of an after-episode interview the cast used that time to perform an a cappella version of "Riu Chiu," a Spanish Christmas carol, in the original Spanish, with Micky singing solo lead on the verses (once again comfortably representing ethnicity) while the others joined in for the chorus. Earlier groups who performed the song include The Kingston Trio (1961) and The Modern Folk Quartet (1964), whose former member, Chip Douglas, had since become the Monkees' music producer and brought them the song. But choosing to do it on television in the original Spanish long before the rise of Telemundo made for a reverential look at a culture not well known across the United States.

Since Mexican Americans were not yet a prominent stereotype in middle America, the writers weren't used to relying on them for humor, whereas most of the largely Jewish writing staff knew the standard jokes associated with other ethnicities, especially Italians since the two immigrant-based ethnic groups often shared neighborhoods in urban centers around the country. *The Godfather* film (1972) made Sicilian gangsters the new metaphors for American cowboys and therefore brought their ethnicity into a more three-dimensional realization that would culminate in *The Sopranos* (1999–2007). Before that two things became habitual, Italians were largely caricaturized in the media as Mafiosi and they were often played by actors of Jewish descent, a practice which had been around since the Jewish Edward G. Robinson played the Italian Caesar Enrico "Rico" Bandello in *Little Caesar* in 1931. These two habits reoccurred in the writing room on *The Monkees* when it came to the episode "Monkees à la Carte" (Gerald Gardner & Dee Caruso and Bernie Orenstein). The episode centered around an Italian restaurant where the band worked as both musicians and waiters and received free food from the congenial, older owner, Pop (played by Paul Rinaldo DeVille, an actor born in Italy). In the teaser the restaurant is taken over by an Italian hood. The audience knows he is an Italian hood because he wears a pinstripe suit, is named after a pasta, Fuselli (Harvey Lembeck), and when Peter asks, "Hey are those guys hoods?" Micky responds, "They're not social workers." Though Jewish, Lembeck played Bilko's sidekick, Corporal Rocco Barbella on Phil Silvers' *Sergeant Bilko* series in the late fifties, making Lembeck a great nephew of Robinson on both series. To compound the "Italian" in "Italian hood," the character's name functions as a homonym to the pasta known more casually as corkscrew pasta. Also, Fuselli's sidekick is named Rocco, a favorite moniker for Italian hoods, though this character is played by an actor neither Jewish nor Italian, Karl Lukas. Finally, the gathering of other crime kingpins at the end of the episode culminates in only the second episode to involve anyone dying, in this case the whole table full of fake Mafiosi kill each other in an (invisible) bloodbath while the band members manage to dodge the spray of bullets. While the perfectly planned mass execution of the enemies of the Corleones in *The Godfather* would not appear in book form until 1969 and as a film until 1972, this type of ending was typical of many gangster films of the 1930s and '40s.

Italian hoods had appeared briefly in the earlier episode, "Your Friendly Neighborhood Kidnappers" when a manager named Trump tries to keep the band from competing against his clients by getting them to agree to be kidnapped as a publicity stunt. Trump says he knows just who to get, "Two actor clients of mine. They play great hoods." When he calls his clients (Vic Tayback and Louis Quinn) they are seen dressed in pin-stripe suits and busy pouring cement into a bucket containing the feet of a kidnapped man. Such characters, one named Rocco yet again, also appeared in "Monkees in the Ring" (Gardner and Caruso) and Micky mimicked another Italian stereotype. When Davy decides to be a boxer to earn some money, Micky plays an elderly, stooping Italian man begging Davy not to fight or he'll never play the violin again. One wonders how many clichés could exist in one sentence. Then in "Monkees at the Circus" the group poses as The Flying Mozzarella Brothers, complete with moustaches and broken English accents, to save the circus. In "Monkee Chow Mein" Mike and Davy go undercover to the Chinese restaurant to spy on the gangsters who have kidnapped Micky and Peter. They disguise themselves as Italian men wearing fedoras and dark moustaches and speak in broken accents, asking for "a mediuma pizza" and "pro-*chu*-to." Likewise, in "Monkees in a Ghost Town" when Micky and Peter want to convince George and Lenny to let Mike and Davy out of jail, Micky goes undercover as the Big Man. Wearing a pinstripe suit and fedoras, Micky talks like Jimmy Cagney but this time the real gangsters do not buy into his impression.

After "Monkees à la Carte" the two episodes featuring the most blatant Italians-as-gangsters stereotypes appeared in "Alias Micky Dolenz" (Gardner, Caruso and Evans) and "Monkees on the Wheel." In "Alias" Micky, the band member, is confronted in a parking lot by yet another Italian in a pinstripe suit, with dark glasses and a last name ending in a vowel, Tony Ferano (Jimmy Murphy, this time an Irishman playing an Italian). Ferano assumes Micky to be "Baby Face," a gangster boss thought to be in prison. Micky goes to the police to report the attack and is mistaken for Baby Face by them as well. When shown a picture of himself in gangster suit and hat, Micky responds, "Whoever he is, he's a sneaky, vicious, mean-type-looking person." Though Ferano is clearly an Italian name, Micky's doppelganger is given a Spanish surname, Morales, yet in costume and attitude he clearly fits the movie cliché of an Italian gangster.

The writers of *The Monkees* were not finished with Italian stereotypes yet. In "Monkees on the Wheel" (Coslough Johnson) Micky accidentally wins money at the Roulette Wheel, which is then stolen from him by the gangsters who rigged the wheel—the Boss (David Astor) and Biggy (Vic Tayback making his second appearance as a hood). The police make them retrieve the stolen money or face twenty years in prison. The Monkees return to the Casino with three dressed as gangsters, the Insidious Strangler (Micky), Muscles the Mauler (Davy) and Vicious Killer (Mike). Peter dresses as a nerdy math professor with a slide rule and a formula for beating the Roulette Wheel. This episode allows Micky once again to do his Jimmy Cagney as gangster imitation and guest actor Astor does both Cagney and Robinson impressions. As always, good guys—in the Monkees' case, typical (though long-haired) American teenagers—beat bad guys, in these multiple cases, Italians.

The show's final look at mobsters who seem to be Italians served as a metatextual message about how the media automatically presented all gangsters as Italians. "The Picture Frame" (Jack Winter) aired as the second episode of the second season and featured a con man convincing Davy, Micky and Mike they were actors portraying bank robbers so that they would unwittingly rob a real bank. The con man casts them as bank bandits. He asks to see "how you look in the part" and the magic of television editing cut to them in costume. Instead of being dressed as Bonnie and Clyde, then newly glamorized as the epitome of young, sexy bank robbers in a film that had premiered just a month earlier and caused a style sensation, the Monkees transform once again into clichéd Tommy-gun-carrying, cigar-chomping (an ode to Al Capone), pinstripe-suit-wearing gangsters. Micky gets one more chance to mimic Jimmy Cagney and the audience gets one more chance to believe Italians are no more than gangsters.

The oddest part of having most Italian characters presented as gangsters and none of them as normal Italian friends populating the world of *The Monkees*, is, as previously mentioned, that Dolenz was essentially Italian. His father, George Dolenz, came from Trieste, Italy (though when the elder Dolenz was born it was still part of Austria-Hungary). Since Micky's character did not conform to any of the broader Italian stereotypes involving accents or criminal activity (and he was only half Italian) did the audience even sense that he was representing that ethnicity?

As far as Asian Americans were concerned, they did not have even a token representation among the lead characters on the show and when appearing as guest characters only appeared in caricature. This began in the typical, metatextual moment in "Dance, Monkees Dance" involving the Writer's Room populated by elderly Chinese men with close-cropped hair and long moustaches. When Micky reads the pages they have supposedly written for the scene and mumbles, "Those guys are really overpaid," he is involved in stereotyping and discriminating both the Chinese writers and all Hollywood writers, a minority in their own right (but that's another chapter), in general. He is not, however, othering them. While a verbal cousin to stereotyping and discriminating, the psychological act of othering goes one step further. To other, one must find a difference in another group of people, judge the difference as making that group inferior and then subjugate that group due to the difference. Chinese Americans had been othered since their first arrival during the California Gold Rush of the 1850s and their subsequent work on the transcontinental railroads. Americans of European descent, who held political power, were able to pass the Chinese Exclusion Act of 1882, effectively banning Chinese immigration and therefore impinging on their finances and their ability to travel and find work.

The next quick view of a Chinese character comes in Season One in "The Case of the Missing Monkee" (written by Gardner and Caruso). When Peter goes missing after a gig at a French restaurant, the remaining band members bring a policeman to the restaurant, which has been transformed into a Chinese restaurant. The villain du jour, Dr. Marcovich, succeeds in fooling the cop by disguising himself as a Chinese waiter, complete with corny accent not accorded to the Chinese writers of "Dance, Monkees, Dance" since those characters never even spoke. In Episode 26 of that season, "Monkees Chow Mein" (also written by Gardner and Caruso) the caricatures populate the entire episode, beginning with the Dragonman who operates a criminal gang in the back room of a Chinese restaurant the Monkees frequent. Despite being of Jewish heritage, actor Joey Forman earned the role of Dragonman after several previous roles caricaturizing Asian stereotypes. Two of those performances were on *Get Smart*, the show writers Gardner and Caruso staffed before *The Monkees*. On *Get Smart* Forman played the recurring character Harry Hoo, a Hawaiian detective parody of Charlie Chan. Later in his career he would release a comedy album with Bill Dana where Forman played the Mashuganishi Yogi, utilizing a fake Indian accent. For his turn as Dragonman, Forman pulled out all the stops. The costume is so extreme that Forman was able to appear as a guest lead just three episodes after having portrayed the completely European American character of television host, Captain Crocodile. As Dragonman, Forman wears the traditional Fu Manchu moustache, a queue (long ponytail down his back) and makeup that reshapes his eyes and yellows his complexion.

While the costumes are extreme, the comedy tried to balance between disrespectful attitudes toward both cultures. When the Chinese gangsters chase the band out of the restaurant and Davy asks why, Mike responds: "Orientals are a curious people." Moments later, when an all-American CIA agent ushers them into his car at gunpoint, Davy asks the same question and Mike makes the matching response: "Occidentals are a curious people." Later, when Dragonman's henchman, Toto, has kidnapped the wrong long-haired Monkee (Micky instead of Peter) his defense is, "All American look alike to me," so he deals out an anti–American attitude, but with a broken English accent. Similarly, when Peter comes to the restaurant to save Micky, Dragonman gleefully rubs his hands and says Pete has "fallen into my crutches." Micky questions, "Your crutches?" and Dragonman responds, "Not my crutches, my crutches" further enhancing the broken English representation.

The only positive representation of Asian culture came unexpectedly in the final episode, "Frodis Caper," co-written by Dolenz and Dave Evans. As discussed in Chapter Two, a Buddhist chant known as the Lotus Sutra aided the band in escaping the evil Wizard Glick and saving the world. Therefore these all-American boys save the world with the help of *nam-myoho-renge-kyo*, a teaching from the first historical Buddha, Siddhartha Gautama. The chant hopes to awaken one's Buddha nature and tap into the deepest levels of our existence, on which our own lives and that of the universe are one. The question to be asked is whether by using the Lotus Sutra chant the effect is to honor or to insult Asian culture. As so many American musicians and other artists of the era who worked and socialized with the actors on the show—and Tork himself—identified as Buddhists, one imagines the chant was treated respectfully. Despite a lack of political correctness in the representation of characters of Asian descent, these last moments of the show left a positive impression of Eastern religion and culture on a new generation of young Americans.

Perhaps due to the attention drawn by the Red Power Movement during the run of *The Monkees*, Native Americans tended to fare better than Americans of Asian descent. Perhaps the fact that Dolenz self-identified as part Native American on his mother's side had an effect. Perhaps the writers were looking to move beyond the Tonto/Lone Ranger dynamic. Or perhaps the writers and actors found a connection between Native Americans and the emerging ideology of the hippie movement. Whatever the causes, the Native Americans are portrayed in a stereotypical visual style—sitting cross-legged (what used to be called "Indian style") outside a teepee and wearing a headdress. Perhaps because the writers didn't know how else to telegraph that these characters were Native Americans to the audience. But these few characters also spoke in a hip, smart style, clearly superior to the "white man" with themes reminiscent of the hippie ideology.

The Monkees first encounter Native Americans as they are trying to escape from gangsters Lenny, George and the Big Woman in the first season's "Monkees in a Ghost Town" (written by Meyerson and Schlitt). In an attempt to escape from the Big Woman (Rose Marie) and her gang, Davy sneaks off to call for help. He reaches an Native American sitting cross-legged in front of a teepee, though his long black hair and multicolored shirt would be equally at home at the Monterey Pop Festival. When Davy explains they are being held prisoner in a ghost town, the Native American identifies himself as a "primitive Indian chief" (though he wears no corresponding feathered headdress) and responds: "Me cannot help. Know nothing about White Man's problems." Davy pleads but the Native American's other phone rings and he puts Davy on hold.

Equally misunderstood due to years of stereotypical portrayals, Romani immigrants, more colloquially known as Gypsies, fell victim to caricature whenever they appeared on *The Monkees* (and any other sitcoms of the 1960s for that matter). Historically, the Romani people emigrated to the United States from several countries in Eastern Europe and refer to themselves with specific names: Romani came from Serbia, Russia and Austria-Hungary and largely worked as coppersmiths though they dabbled in fortune-telling; Ludar or Romanian Gypsies from Bosnia largely worked in carnivals and circuses; Romnichels came from England and worked as horse traders and basket weavers. There are other subgroups but it is clear that writers took elements of each group to create the basic set of gypsy characters found interacting with the Monkees. Such characters first appeared in season 1, episode 15 "Too Many Girls" (written by Dave Evans, Gerald Gardner and Dee Caruso). When the Samantha Stevens–like appearance of random women distracts Davy from rehearsing "(I'm Not Your) Stepping Stone," his bandmates take him to a Gypsy Tea Room for a break from the distractions of women. There Mrs. Badderly, a mother who is more Mama Rose than gypsy (played by Reta Shaw) schemes to have Davy quit the group to become her talentless daughter's partner in a televised amateur talent show. It only needed to be a Gypsy Tea Room rather than an English Tea Room so that the mother could read their tea leaves and predict that Davy would leave the group for love. Shaw, herself from Maine, and her daughter Fern (played by Ohioan Kelly Jean Peters) were visually WASP descendants of the Mayflower rather than ethnic Eastern European immigrants. In fact, actress Reta Shaw had been seared into movie-goers minds as the perfectly proper English maid due to her performance as "The Domestic" alongside perpetually English Hermione Baddeley in 1964 in *Mary Poppins*. After her work on *The Monkees,* Shaw would play the housekeeper, Martha Grant, on the television version of *The Ghost and Mrs. Muir* from 1968 to 1970. Here she serves as an example of the white-washing caused when casting directors cast white actors as ethnic characters, a practice still existing into the next millennium.

In the very next week's episode, "The Son of a Gypsy" (written by Gerald Gardner, Dee Caruso and Treva Silverman), this visual confusion was cured by the casting of Jeanne Arnold as gypsy mother Maria. Though Arnold was not of Eastern European descent either, her hair was darkened and the costuming enhanced the idea of her being a gypsy through the use of a head scarf and an abundance of jangling gold costume jewelry. Her three sons are also attired in loosely-fitting silk garments and gold earrings. She further identifies them as gypsies when she says, "We do not want you to think that gypsies are a vengeful people," after the Monkees get the gig they were all auditioning for at the home of Madame Rantha. Then her son Marco (played by Vincent Beck) bites off the head of a nail and she calms him down and invites the Monkees to visit them at their camp so they can see that "gypsies know how to laugh." All this happens in the Teaser. As the story unfolds we learn that the gypsies had wanted the gig in order to steal the precious Maltese Vulture from Madame Rantha.[7] Being denied that chance, they intend to force the Monkees to do the job by kidnapping Peter. This involves many other stereotypes of gypsies including knife throwing, fortune telling, and kidnapping.

While gypsies never appeared again so blatantly, their cousins in stereotyping, the Russians, did appear. The two seasons of the show fell in the middle of the Cold War, post the Cuban Missile Crisis but long before the fall of the Berlin Wall. "The Spy Who Came in from the Cool" arrived as the first season's fifth episode, the title parody taken from the John le Carré novel, which was adapted for the screen by Paul Dehn and Guy Trosper in 1965. The story, written by Gerald Gardner and Dee Caruso again parodying famous films, involves Davy buying a new pair of red maracas within which spies have stored some microfilm. To retrieve the microfilm, Madame and Boris go undercover as hippies to a club where The Monkees are playing and Madame succeeds in stealing back the microfilm. At the end the C.I.S. agent says, "Madame got away. She's probably on her way to Red China by now," making the stereotypical assumption that all Russians were Communist Party members. The next scene declares itself to take place "Somewhere in China" where Madame announces to a room full of cigar-smoking, Chinese spies (another small slap at that culture) that her microfilm shows a new weapon of modern warfare. Alas for her, it is in fact a music video starring The Monkees singing "Saturday's Child." As each of the spies leaves the secret room, Madame sinks to the floor in embarrassment.

Since Gardner and Caruso had cut their writing teeth on television's number one spy parody, *Get Smart*, "The Spy Who Came in from the Cool" tended to involve more homages to Buck Henry's series buried within than stereotypes of Russians. Mostly that came from the characterizations of the two Russian spies. Arlene Martel as Madame had already played three different Russian females on *Hogan's Heroes* and clearly played ethnic so well she was cast as the farthest thing from an American–T'Pring, the Vulcan bride of the alien Mr. Spock, in "Amok Time" on *Star Trek*. The casting director on *The Monkees* liked her so much she returned the next season to play Lorelai in "Monstrous Monkee Mash." Her partner in crime, Boris, was not played by an actor or Russian descent either. Jacques Aubuchon, a Massachusetts native of French Canadian descent, portrayed Boris, as well as many a Russian character in an acting career that spanned from the early 1950s to the late 1980s.

Russians became the focus again in "The Card Carrying Red Shoes" (written by Treva Silverman using the pseudonym Lee Sanford). Though their country uses a pseudonym as well, Druvania, the characters all exhibit negative Russian stereotypes beginning with being spies who have gone undercover as ballerinas bearing names like Natasha Pavlova (Ondine Vaughn), Ivan (Vincent Beck) and Nicolai (Leon Askin). Natasha discusses defecting to America, Ivan discusses microfilm and Nicolai discusses kidnapping. Later in the episode, when Micky and Davy need to go undercover, they choose to dress as Cossacks, appropriate to the Russian aesthetic of the episode as the Cossacks are most known for destroying pogroms and suppressing revolutionaries as the Tsars' police. While dressed as Cossacks Micky and Davy are asked to demonstrate their agility at Russian dancing, not Druvanian dancing.

Perhaps the minority the audience least expected to see on the show, the elderly, fared best in that each time an elderly character appeared the Monkees actively worked to keep that character from being exploited by a middle-aged villain. It was as if the two ends of the generational spectrum needed each other to survive the generation gap. In "I've Got a Little Song Here" (written by Treva Silverman) Mike receives a letter offering to purchase his songs. He goes to the High Class Music Publishing Company with the song "I'm Gonna Buy Me a Dog" (actually written by the Monkees in-house songwriters Tommy Boyce and Bobby Hart). The company turns out to be a scam run by middle-aged Bernie Class (Phil Leeds). The Monkees don't just help Mike get his money back. They also spend time helping an elderly man (82-year-old Owen McGiveney) Mike met in the Teaser by retrieving his money as well.

In "Monkee Mayor" (written by Jack Winter) three elderly neighbors (Peter Brocco, Violet Carlson and Queenie Smith) tell the Monkees they are all being evicted by the city so their homes can be paved over for a parking lot.[8] Both the sitting mayor (Irwin Charone) and the construction tsar (Monty Landis who will return as the Devil in "The Devil and Peter Tork") are greedy, middle-aged capitalists taking advantage of the elderly. The Monkees solve the problem by having Mike run for Mayor to rectify the situation, but he gets into campaign financing trouble through his trusting nature. Mike's eventual television speech of apology mimics Nixon's Checkers speech from 1952 until Mike announces his withdrawal from the race. When it looks like our heroes will fail, Mike's speech succeeds in making the sitting mayor apologize on camera for being controlled by moneyed interests and promises to do better in the future. The parking lot conspiracy is destroyed and the Monkees' neighbors can move back into their own homes.

In "A Coffin Too Frequent" (written by Stella Linden[9]) the Monkees manage to save the day (or in this case the night) for one of television's most iconic elderly characters, played by comedian Ruth Buzzi. Though she was 31 years old at the time of her guest appearance, making her only a decade older than the regular cast, Buzzi would make a career of portraying little old lady characters. Her best known, park bench-sitting spinster Gladys Ormphby, would appear later that year on *Rowan and Martin's Laugh-In*. Buzzi warmed up for it here on *The Monkees* playing Mrs. Milfred Weatherspoon in an episode that once again allowed the teenagers to save an elderly character from a middle-aged scam artist who promised to raise her husband from the dead right in the Monkees' living room. Her age is communicated to us visually, in her white wig; verbally in dialogue such as Micky announcing, "She's a nice little old lady and I'm not gonna stand here and see her get her money taken away from her"; and in stereotypical little old lady actions such as sending Peter to bed when he sneezes, forcing him to drink tea, taking his temperature and wrapping him in a cellophane tent as was done to children with pneumonia in that era. She is not weak, however, as is demonstrated when she hits Micky over the head with her umbrella before he can open the coffin and disturb her husband before the séance.

Interestingly, all the elderly episodes concern the middle-aged generation trying to take advantage of the elderly. Yet while the elderly characters are clearly a bit naïve, they also all live independently, take care of their normal daily business well, and none of them suffer from any long term illnesses, as elderly characters seem to have done more frequently in the later television seasons. Overall, it seems that the phrase coined by free speech activist Jack Weinberger in 1964—"Don't trust anyone over 30"—on *The Monkees* might have included—but do trust anyone over 80.[10]

Overall the coverage and treatment of minorities on *The Monkees* fluctuated based on the then current cultural conversation created by each different minority, resulting in African Americans finally growing out of their Jim Crow caricatures thanks to the prominence of the Civil Rights Movement. Meanwhile, televised versions of Italian and Chinese characters were relegated to twirling pasta and Fu Manchu mustaches for another decade or so.

Six

We Were Made for Each Other
The Menagerie of Metatextuality

Among the many technical terms students confront when studying the aesthetics of television, the one they seem to remember most is metatextuality, which in laymen's terms happens when a character breaks the fourth wall with an aside to the audience, thereby acknowledging that someone, the audience, is watching and admitting they know they are playing a character in a fictional world. The term dates to Molière and before, when proscenium theatres had three solid walls around the action and that fourth invisible wall between them and the audience. Shakespearean characters such as Iago in *Othello* break the fourth wall often and it is a stylistic choice writers have made ever since. In this, *The Monkees* follows a long tradition of television programs that relied heavily on this aesthetic device to create both humor and that sense of fun endemic to the program while also fostering that anti-authority attitude mentioned in Chapter Two, on the way the show transmitted counterculture messages. Past television programs that relied on metatextuality include comedies such as *The George Burns and Gracie Allen Show* (which also shared the concept of using the actors' real names for their onscreen characters with *The Monkees*), *Malcolm in the Middle,* and dramatic programs such as *House of Cards*. Because metatextuality refuses to take for granted how stories should be told it comments on the nature of fiction itself and plays with how stories can be told. It is this technique, along with their physical slapstick, that likely clinched *The Monkees* the Emmy for Outstanding Comedy Series in 1967.

Metatextuality was not alone among the techniques used by the various writers, directors and editors of the series. Many felt themselves to be among the same "young generation" mentioned in the theme song and relished experimenting in a medium that was then only a decade old itself. Others, such as prop man Jack Williams and make up supervisor Ben Lane were old hands in production. While reports are that some were annoyed by the frantic antics of the young cast, others clearly enjoyed the new energy *The Monkees* provided them for their careers, and the acknowledgement that came from frequent appearances in front of the camera during improv moments or during the Christmas episode which ended with the cast introducing a line-up of crew members on camera to the home audience. Costume and set designers and art directors added wildly mixed colors not often used in television, in an era when many audience members still owned black and white television sets. Likewise, film editors sped up or slowed down the film as well as intercutting old footage for humorous effects in the same way sound editors intercut inappropriate sounds into scenes. This all added up to a new, exciting aesthetic that caught the eye of a newer viewer and was planned from the start by the producers. In an interview with *TV Week,* Rafelson claimed he was creating "something rare in television–creativity, freedom and non-phoniness.... We're doing something new, avoiding the status quo. We're probably the only show with the technical crew built around the content. I interviewed lighting men, cameramen, and soundmen. Writers and directors, too. Most of them are young, but the main thing is they had to be involved, had to have an eagerness to swing with the inventive style of the show."[1]

TV Guide, once the bible helping viewers make choices for their fall premiere season, recognized Rafelson's style choices as setting the show apart. In their announcement of the program they wrote:

> *The Monkees* is coming. And win, lose or draw, it's a series which, at least, is different. The premise is conventional enough.... The difference is in the way the show is done. Just as its four leading men are patterned on The Beatles, its production techniques are borrowed in large measure from The Beatles' movies. The whole thing is played within a nontraditional framework with frenetic changes of costume and scene, slapstick chases, photographic pranks of all sorts.

Urban myth across the decades declared the show's style to be a direct descendant of The Beatles film *A Hard Day's Night* (1964). In an article given after Jones' death, co-creator Bob Rafelson refuted that idea. "This was a show I had written six years before the Beatles existed, and the pilot was based on my own life as an itinerant musician when I was 17 years old. What The Beatles did was to create a kind of permission for any rock 'n' roll to be a popular subject for television."[2] In an oral history interview with David Polad, one of the writers of the pilot, Paul Mazursky refuted Rafelson's refutation and brought credit for the style of the program back to himself and Larry Tucker who had been staff writers on *The Danny Kaye Show* when hired to do *The Monkees*. "We were considered hot— they came in and wanted to do a show like the Beatles, like *Help* … jazzy and crazy and kooky … they [Rafelson and Schneider] certainly were influential but we wrote that zip, cut, bang, whack. We're responsible for ruining everything with the MTV style."[3]

In the pilot, the mere act of including the unrehearsed auditions of Jones and Nesmith ushered in the underlying metatextuality almost by accident. It was actually a desperate attempt to raise the ratings of the test audience who complained they could not tell the difference between the four long-haired band members. This act was the work of Rafelson who as producer had the final edit approval. After those two auditions, Mazursky and Tucker employed the disembodied narrator, sounding a bit like a *Twilight Zone* set up, to tell the audience, "Well, those are some of the Monkees and you never know when they'll turn up next." Here the pilot writers created guest spots for themselves and the zippy, new, faster editing entered *The Monkees* with a smash cut to pilot writer Paul Mazursky, playing the Man on the Street interviewer, cornering co-writer Larry Tucker, playing an upstanding elder in the community. From here on in the combination of writing and editing shows how much editors are the final rewrite team on any episode of television. In this six-minute teaser, Tucker's character insists if ever he saw violence perpetrated in the streets, he would assist the victims. Then he is presented with the long-haired Monkees pummeling their shortest member, Davy, who cries out for help. Rather than assist, Tucker's character races away, illustrating the cynicism and hypocrisy young Americans felt best described their elders. This is followed by fast edits across the musical title sequence of the band members in various visually stimulating locations from Kiddieland to the beach.

The opening credits end on a relic of the silent film age, a title card reading "Whew!" directly thanking the audience for surviving the fast ride through introducing the main actors. As if to offer the audience some assistance, the second card reads, "And Now for Our Story." These title cards function both as metatext and as a means to make older viewers more comfortable with the otherwise modern pace of the program. Then the promised story involves the band auditioning to play for Vanessa Russell's Sweet 16 party. Upon meeting, the special effect (such as they were in the 1960s) of stars twinkling in Davy and Vanessa's eyes, accompanied by the sound effects of a strumming harp and chirping birds, serve as metaphors for falling in love and function to tell the audience they are watching a love story. As the band begins to play, what might be called the first MTV video is created. The camera dollies up to Vanessa and Davy's faces, then the original pilot cuts to another title card "As the Boys Play On, Davy Dreams" which brings the audience into a fast paced collection of shots of Davy and Vanessa romping in the woods while the band plays perched in a statuesque California oak. (In the aired pilot, that title card was cut, probably on the belief that having the camera zoom into Davy's eyes was enough to insinuate what came next was his dream. This seems to show that the producers credited the audience with enough time in front of filmed stories to understand the shorthand of the dolly shot of someone's eyes.) Next all four band members race into a closed down Kiddieland where they engage in sped up film moments playing all the carnival games and rides. Davy's dream ends as he and Vanessa are being photographed in old western wedding attire. It fades out on Vanessa handcuffing him and smiling maniacally. Coming out of the dream the band is hired (another dream realized) and a jump cut finds Davy and Vanessa standing outside her front door at the end of a date.

Another written title card appears (connecting the writers to their silent screen ancestors who were called title writers rather than screenwriters) after Vanessa enters her house, "But Inside All Is Not Well." The next quick edit comes after Vanessa promises her parents that despite staying out until 1am (a teenager's true dream for a school night curfew), "I'll pass my history final." The screen flips to her in a new costume, illustrating it is the next day, admitting she flunked her history final. As soon as she announces the fact that she can take a make-up exam the screen does another flip to the character of Jill, standing on the beach telling the Monkees that if Vanessa flunks this make up exam they will lose the chance to play at her party. This scene morphs into the second MTV style video of Davy walking on the beach trailed by a toddler, worried about the problem he has caused Vanessa. The slower version of Davy singing "I Wanna Be Free" plays over his walk. When Mike says they need to hold a board meeting to handle the situation, he bangs his gavel on the table and instantly the four teenagers are wearing business suits instead of the casual clothes they had sat down wearing. This is followed by a montage of the

Monkees singing about and enacting moments in history for Vanessa to remember, which she does.

Costume changes come further into play as the band tries to sneak into the country club. As they jump over the wall they are suddenly wearing 1930s style prison uniforms. In the chase that ensues, the audience sees them in western garb and wearing chimpanzee masks, playing on the monkey joke that eventually grew old and disappeared but was a frequent focus in early episodes. The final musical romp, to the tune "Let's Dance On" focuses on wild shots of teenage dancers à la American Bandstand, a show which had been ingrained in the minds of television-watching teenagers since its debut in 1952. The frame freezes on one teenage girl dancing the twist with a dialogue bubble that reads, "A Typical Teenager?" A few beats later that bubble is changed to, "No, a friend of the producer!" This highlights the youthful ideas that adults are not to be trusted and nothing is as it seems in life or in this new-fangled program.

As Rafelson and Mazursky each claimed a slice, it is likely this visual and verbal concept came from a combination of both entities, creating the first flush of free-wheeling frivolity that would define the program across its run. Then the task of maintaining it on a weekly basis fell to the staff writers. As discussed in Chapter Three, the writers planned much of the mayhem by virtue of the plots they created for each episode. These writers wrote a good deal of the metatextuality into their scripts, understanding it to be the voice of the show. Often these Shakespearean asides included comments on the current plot or the craft of writing in general and sometimes they inserted nods to the work of their fellow television writers. Though the pilot filmed first, it did not air first. Peter Meyerson and Robert Schlitt opened the first season with "Royal Flush" which gave Micky's character the first chance to be seen by the audience demonstrating breaking the fourth wall. When the evil henchman, Sigmund, (via help from the editors) jumps from a chair into a doorway, Micky does a double take, then addresses the audience with, "He's fast!"

This is the beginning of a trend of the writers assigning these metatextual moments more often to Micky, perhaps because his character was meant as comic relief and perhaps because, as a professional actor coming into the series they assumed he could manage them best. Or naturally in their minds he 'knew' the business best and could therefore report on it to the audience. In "The Spy Who Came in from the Cool" when the Monkees are trying to secretly record a confession from Russian spies, they encounter several technical difficulties. By the fourth attempt Micky has taken a clapper-board off the floor, snapped it and said directly to the camera "Spy confession Take 4." A few weeks later in "The Chaperone" Davy tries to meet a woman by going door to door as a pollster asking, "What television program are you watching?" After the woman goes inside and the rest of the band race up to see how he did, Peter asks naively "What TV show was she watching?" Micky's answer, to the camera as much as to his bandmates: "Ours, I hope." Then when they realize that the woman only goes out to chaperoned parties Micky and Davy do a double take to the audience and repeat "chaperoned parties," as if sharing their lightbulb moment with their viewers. At the very end of this mash-up of *Charley's Aunt* and *Some Like It Hot*, where Micky has been unmasked as the fake female chaperone that the general has fallen in love with, Micky asks the audience, "Do I have to give back the ring?" By episode 18, "I Was a Teenage Monster," Micky finds the evil scientist's daughter in the bedroom closet. She claims she won't be needed until the sequel. When he opens he same door later in the show she is found reading a green-covered *Monkees* script. Micky asks her what she thinks about her father's behavior and she promises, "Wait until you see the sequel. A vampire turns Davy into a werewolf," properly predicting what will happen in the second season, episode 50 "The Monstrous Monkee Mash."

Dolenz's knowledge of the inner world of television became fodder for much metatextuality, including the Chinese writers on the Underwoods bit invented by freelance writer Bernie Orenstein in "Dance, Monkees Dance." In "Monkees Get Out More Dirt" Peter needs to ask, "How do I get in if the door's locked?" Micky replies, "Peter, you can't expect the writers to know everything. Improvise." Five minutes into episode seven, "Monkees in Ghost Town" Peter updates Micky on what Micky already knows: "First we got lost and run out of gas, then Mike and Davy disappear and somebody starts shooting off a machine gun and now this guy is searching the town." Micky looks directly into the camera and says, "That's for the benefit of any of you who tuned in late. Now back to our story." This comment referenced a common issue in the days before the invention of VCRs, DVRs allowed viewers to time-shift and binge-watch in that often viewers would tune in late and need to be given some creative way to catch up with the story. Writers found ways to reprise the story, usually after a commercial break, and this is what Meyerson and Schlitt chose to do via parody.

The most meta of all Micky's moments came when referencing his past as a child actor on *Circus Boy* in episode 22 "Monkees at the Circus" (written by David Panich). Though the episode did not employ any asides at all, it found another way to tease the audience. The episode opens with Micky saying, "I haven't been to the circus since I was a kid." Then he adlibs, "Reminds me of when I was a boy." Later in the show he sings snippets of the *Circus Boy* theme song. When Mike asks what he is singing, Micky says, "It's an old TV series." Dolenz was also recognized as a former child actor in the produced version of the song "I'm Gonna Buy Me a Dog" by Tommy Boyce and Bobby Hart which appeared in episode 12 "I've Got a Little Song Here." In the recording studio Jones and Dolenz began improvising dialogue. At one point Dolenz said, "But I could teach a dog to do that" and Jones sang back, "You can't teach dogs to do that. You can only train elephants."

More typical meta moments for Micky include the shoot-out in Pop's restaurant in the end of "Monkees à la Carte" when Micky makes them pause for a woman in a fur coat to walk through the scene showing off her outfit. After she exits Micky turns to the camera and says, "The director thought we should have a pretty girl in the show." During Peter's trial in "Devil and Peter Tork" when the boys insist the prosecution call another witness, the judge asks, "On what grounds?" Micky responds, "On the grounds that the television show isn't over yet." In "Monkees Race Again" (written by Dave Evans, Elias Davis and David Pollock) the actor playing T. N. Crumpets (William Glover) is gagged so he has minimal dialogue. Micky adlibs "Boy you sure got a lousy part" first. Then when a second gag is placed in Crumpets' mouth and Micky elaborates, "You flew all the way to Hollywood for this part?"

Though Micky managed most such moments, the style scattered across the rest of the cast as needed. Just a few episodes into season one, in "Too Many Girls" (written by Dave Evans) when Mike, Micky and Peter realize Fern is the tea leaf lady's daughter, they all do a take to the camera to repeat "Her *daughter* and Davy." Later, when Davy learns the same thing, he will get the same take to the camera as he repeats "Her *daughter*?" Later in the story, when the Amateur Hour breaks for "A word from our sponsor," Peter, Mike and Micky question, "They're sponsor?" and assert for the audience, "Our sponsor." In a deeper bit of metatextuality, one that does not involve obviously breaking the fourth wall but another wink to the audience, when Mike performs alone on the Amateur Hour he plays a sped up version of "Different Drum," a song the fans knew he had written and the Stone Poneys (featuring Linda Ronstadt) had recorded. Many of Mike's asides came from his position as father figure. In "I was a Teenage Monster" when Peter uses the phrase "avaricious ambitions" Mike questions those words, asking Davy "Where'd he get that?" Davy answers, "It's in the script." Mike is still hesitant, "Are you sure?" "Yeah, it's on page 28." One adlib perfectly crafted for Davy came in "Monkees in the Ring." Davy takes up boxing and when a reporter asks him, "What fight was most important to you?" he responds, "The Revolutionary War." Then in an aside to the camera he continues, "That's when we gave you this little island. No letters on that, please."

Jones' stage experience put him in the center of several meta moments as well. In "Monstrous Monkee Mash" Davy to the Wolfman, "What you need is a good agent. These people are exploiting you." Later, when someone asks the Wolfman what he wants, Davy answers for him, "He wants a better percentage of the profits. He wants cookouts on the weekends. He wants to play his own music." This last "want" is a deeper play on the then current issue the actor/musicians were having with the producers about recording an album on their own. In "Hillbilly Honeymoon" when the Monkees get into yet more trouble, Micky asks what they can do to get out of it. Mike pulls out an actual script. They read lines from it and Davy asks if his reading was dramatic enough. In "Case of the Missing Monkee" (written by Gardner and Caruso) the trio bring a policeman to the French restaurant where they saw Peter disappear, but it has now been altered to resemble an Asian locale, with the weekly villain succeeding in fooling the cop in his disguise as a Chinese waiter. As they leave the restaurant, Davy turns to the camera and says, "You know, I never did like Chinese restaurants. An hour after you eat there, you disappear." Later in the episode, while searching for Peter, the phone rings and Mike answers. He gives the details of all the events that took place before hanging up. When Micky wonders if it was police on the phone Mike says, "No, it was *TV Guide.*"

"Captain Crocodile" (Gardner, Caruso, Meyerson & Schlitt) captured the behind the scenes, real life drama growing between the producers and the actors/musicians, thinly disguised as a send-off of the beloved children's program host Captain Kangaroo combined with the urban myth of a children's television show host who actually hated children and eventually signed off with the line, "There, that oughta hold the little bastards."

While Captain Kangaroo existed (and was on the air for 29 years) folklore historians have debunked the second story across the years. No children's program host ever uttered that phrase.[4] Perhaps the Monkee staff writers had heard that myth and wove it into this episode, thereby furthering its reach as a popular culture urban myth. The episode involves the Monkees being booked to perform on the "Captain Crocodile" television show but instead of being allowed to play their music, pies are thrown at them. The audience recognizes the story will be a farce when it echoes the Wasteland Speech given by FCC Chairman Newton Minow in 1961. As the band enters the TV studio Micky says, "So this is the world of television" to which Peter replies, "That's funny. It doesn't look like a vast wasteland."[5]

The writers of "Captain Crocodile" even spoofed the producer who hired them. Bert Schneider had sold *The Monkees* to Columbia Studios where his father Abe was president. For "Captain Crocodile" the writers created a ten-year old network executive who called the president of the network "Dad." A deeper dig at the studio establishment came later in the show when the band insisted on being able to actually sing during the "Captain Crocodile" show. This episode filmed and aired as the relationship between the band and music producer Don Kirshner grew more volatile over the question of who would choose the music they recorded. In this episode the pint-sized executive guarantees the band that "there will be no more pies in the face and you WILL sing." Later, when the boys are reading to the children in the audience, their story takes place in the mythical "Land of Kirshner."

The writers and producers also took the time to spoof other programs on the air in the late 1960s, some produced by parent company Screen Gems and some with ties to the writers. During "The Spy Who Came in from the Cool" Davy rubs the table lamp and a blonde genie similar to Barbara Eden of *I Dream of Jeannie* (1965–70) comes out of a puff of smoke saying, "Do not fear, Master. Your genie will help you." Davy shrugs and replies, "Imagine that. Wrong show." In "Monkees Get Out More Dirt" the hand that reaches out of the white box to take the phone from Micky and tries to pull him back down into it is based on Thing of *The Addams Family* (ABC, 1964–66). Also in that episode, Mike pulls off his shoe and uses it as a phone, an homage to *Get Smart* (NBC/CBS, 1965–70) which is where Gardner and Caruso began their sitcom careers. In "Monkees Blow Their Minds" Burgess Meredith can be glimpsed in the nightclub audience wearing his Penguin costume from *Batman* (1966–68). Finally,

Peter climbs a telephone pole, echoing Eddie Albert's city-slicker character, Oliver Wendell Douglass, on *Green Acres* (CBS, 1965–71).

Clearly, the writers and actors relished winking at the world in which they existed, sharing their own exuberance and sense of wonder at the luck of landing in such a life with the audience through sometimes written and sometimes improvised moments within a story. In the opening episode of season two, "A Nice Place to Visit" (written by Treva Silverman) when Peter does the classic western gunman trick of deftly spinning a gun in his hand Mike says, "That's very cool. I didn't know you could do that—you usually play the dummy." That line connects directly to the writer as Silverman always regretted voting for the Peter character to be the dummy rather than the smart nerd. Later in the episode, when Micky prepares for a gunfight by donning a completely white outfit down to the hat, Peter asks, "Are you scared?" Micky says, "No, I'm not scared. I'll welcome this duel. The symbol of good against the symbol of evil and I know I'm gonna be the victor." Davy replies, "Because the symbol of good always wins?" and Micky responds, "No because the lead in a television series always wins." During this episode Silverman also injects a bit of popular culture trivia by having Micky use the phrase, "Badges? We don't need no stinkin' badges." That line, a paraphrase from *The Treasure of the Sierra Madre* (1948), would eventually make it to #36 on the American Film Institute's list "100 Years … 100 Movie Quotes" compiled in 2005. Its use in this 1967 episode of *The Monkees* is credited in popular culture mythology with bringing the quote to a younger, hipper audience and keeping it alive long enough to be re-used by Andrew Bergman and Mel Brooks in *Blazing Saddles* (1974).

In the episode "The Card-Carrying Red Shoes" (Treva Silverman) they admit they are in a TV show—in fact they admit they are in their very own TV show—when Micky has to go undercover as a ballerina in a chicken costume (in an homage to *Swan Lake)*. As Davy is waving the orange chicken costume around, Micky repeats, "I don't want to be a chicken," several times. At the end of that rant he does a take to the audience and speaks into a glass as if it is a walkie-talkie, "Ward, I don't want to be a chicken" which is Micky talking directly to the program's co-producer Ward Sylvester. This addition was likely the work of the actor improvising the producer's name and the director keeping that cut in the final version of the edited program whereas writer Coslough Johnson wrote many metatextual moments into his season two script for "Monkees on the Wheel." When they discuss how to spend the money Micky has won at the roulette wheel, Mike says they have to invest it on something worthwhile. Peter responds in an English accent, "You must be joking." Davy then says, "That's my line" and repeats it in his own English accent after which Peter says, "I'm sorry" in the same accent. When Della the maid comes into their hotel room as they are counting their money, the Monkees make much fuss over her. Davy interrupts the fuss to say, "Wait, she has a line. She has a line." Then Della says, "No," and Davy says, "You don't have a line?" and pushes her out of the shot gently. In one metatextual joke an extra playing a thug pulls Mike's nose and calls him Wizard Glick. Mike says, "I'm not Wizard Glick" and the tormentor turns away. This is a reference to "Frodis Caper" where Rip Taylor, who plays the roulette wheel operator in the current episode, will play a character named Wizard Glick. But the audience hasn't seen that episode yet so the humor is meta-meta. After catching the crooks, Mike, Peter and Davy re-enter the hotel room set and Mike addresses the camera. "Now then, for all practical purposes, the show is over but we have in the television industry what they call a tag which is some sort of just complete laugh riot at the end of a show so that you all tune back in next week. Now the tag we're going to do this week is called a 'Here We Go Again' tag and Davy and Peter are going to do it, it involves Micky." Then we cut to Davy and Peter doing a scene about how none of this would have happened if Micky (to whom they do a fast cut to standing in the casino—and back from) hadn't got the gambling bug. Then Peter says they surely won't get involved in gambling ever again and every time he references Micky, the editors cut to that same shot. Then Mike narrates that, "Now is time to cut over to Micky," and the audience sees him playing with a gambling machine. Mike continues, "Then cut back to us" a couple of times and ends with, "And we're supposed to give a pained look to the camera. Isn't that funny, kids?" Then Mike breaks up laughing while Peter and Davy share the requisite pained looks. This was a particularly short episode as they ended with this tag, then the song "Cuddly Toy" and then outtakes from "Monstrous Monkee Mash" which would air four weeks later. The outtakes involve Mike in mummy attire who keeps breaking up while Micky repeats, "That's a nice button, what does it say?" It takes Mike seven takes before he can straighten up long enough to complete his line, "Save the Texas Prairie Chicken."

As the show was winding down this second season, the occasions for recognizing themselves as actors in a television program, often referenced as being trapped inside the program, become more pronounced, giving evidence of the growing conflict between the artists and the front offices of the studio and network. In "Monstrous Monkee Mash" (written by Neil Nephew and David Panich) after Micky does a scare the audience hears director Jim Frawley's off screen voice say, "Alright, good," an event that would normally be cut. Then Dolenz drops into professional actor mode and says, "Would you like a little bit bigger? That was my medium scare. Would you like a smaller one?" Frawley says, "All right, do a smaller one." Then Dolenz becomes Micky again and does a smaller scare sound. Frawley approves and they continue the scene, never editing their director/actor exchange out of the show. This is a solid example of a metatextual moment created through improvisation between the actor and director on the set, without the intervention of a writer. Later in the episode the writers have their moment. When Micky is frightened in the haunted house and begs Mike to leave, Mike says, "We can't leave now, man, we haven't found Davy." Micky responds, "We could form a trio." Then they enter the room where they left Peter and do a take to the audience, both saying, "He's gone!" Micky immediately responds, "Maybe make it a duet?" Again Mike refuses and Micky says, "If you get lost I'll be a single," followed by singing their theme song as a solo, "Hey, Hey I'm a Monkee." Yet later Davy in his vampire outfit talks to Micky, in Wolfman attire, about how there ought to be a woman in a horror film. After Micky howls, a cute woman comes into the basement and he says, "They don't call me Wolfman for nothing." Then they hear a noise. Davy says, "Someone's coming. Someone's coming" and Micky responds, "Don't be silly. This is a fantasy sequence."

Perhaps the show's boldest comment concerning television came near the end of their run in episode 52 "The Devil and Peter Tork" (Kaufman and Gardner and Caruso). In visualizing hell as the place Peter may be sent since he sold his soul for the ability to play the harp, every time they say "Hell" they are bleeped. This elicits the comment from Micky, "You know what's even more scary? You can't say (bleep) on television." These young writers, actors and producers were clearly engaging this relatively new medium by sharing its quirks and craft and taking the audience inside in a way that even George Burns, by talking directly to the audience, never did. These artists were creating their own world inside the relatively new world created by television.

Seven

We Were Made for Each Other, the Sequel
Television Aesthetic Technique

While metatextuality is largely the work of the writers and actors, the examples in the previous chapter also represent the work of many of the other creative craft departments involved in producing a television show, beginning with directors, editors, properties masters and costumers, all hand-picked by producers Schneider and Rafelson.

The show even involved detailed work from the transportation department in the form of the design and creation of the Monkeemobile by Dean Jeffries, who had already created the Mantaray for *Bikini Beach* and Black Beauty for *The Green Hornet*.

All craft people relied on each other in a show with this much innovation. Directors might ask for actors to perform at a faster pace but then it was through working together with the editor(s) that they were able to speed up those scenes by judicial cutting and, in the case of *The Monkees*, often the insertion of humorous old film footage such as crumbling buildings or exploding volcanoes to match a moment of dialogue. Likewise, writers detailed some of the crazy props the actors could find on set, yet when they asked for a collection of odd kitchen gadgets, it fell to the prop master to decide exactly what those gadgets were, making prop masters key contributors to the creative potential of the production. Similarly, actors can make all the funny faces they like to the camera for comedic effect, but the clothes the costume designers made for them helped add to the hilarity. Special effects being what they were in the days before CGI, they were used less frequently and mostly came in the form of on-screen graphics of light bulbs drawn over Micky's head to suggest a new idea (which happened both in "Your Friendly Neighborhood Kidnappers" and

"Monkees in a Ghost Town"). In these and many other ways the craft departments contributed to the metatextual menagerie. This chapter will detail those contributions.

After the writers who created much of the chaos on the page, the directors were necessary for providing a comfortable and safe surrounding for the actors to practice the brand of improvisation taught to them by actor and first time director, James Frawley (who would win the Emmy for Directing the first season and be nominated three more times in his career for *The Monkees, Ally McBeal* and *Ed*). Frawley trained the actors in similar ways that other comedy troops learn improvisation and then budgeted time on the set for them to create some new physical and verbal comic bits that could be blocked into the actual filming. Peter Tork, reflecting on directing the episode "Monkees Mind Their Manor" on his Facebook post of November 4, 2014, remembered, "We almost never improvised on camera. We would improvise in rehearsals and if it worked we'd repeat it for the camera."

Even more than working with actors, the directors spent time with the editors who brought the next level of metatextuality to the show by cutting in old studio footage and leaving in, with permission of the writers, directors and producers, the blooper moments regularly saved for a gag reel to be shown privately at the end-of-season cast party. Likewise, these film editors under the guidance of directors, sped up or slowed down the film as well as intercutting old footage for humorous effects in the same way sound editors intercut inappropriate sounds into scenes. These inclusions helped create the wild, crazy tone of the program and perhaps most especially gave the young audience the feeling that they were being included in a back stage world heretofore closed to them. Including old studio footage has become a style staple used to great effect by *The Monkees* and to great critical acclaim by the first series to put pay channel HBO on the map, *Dream On* (1990–1996). For that show the producers admitted old footage equaled lower costs to creating *Dream On* and it accidentally became the signature look of the show.

The same could be said for *The Monkees*, where the judicious use of quick cuts began with the pilot and bad audience test data. Apparently when given to a test audience, the pilot rated lower than any other possible pilot for the then upcoming 1966–67 television season. In fact, it was the worst test of any pilot in the history of NBC.[1] The network, NBC, gave the producers one night to make one more attempt at creating a new pilot.

There was no time for rewriting or re-filming anything, so re-editing (re-cutting the existing filmed material) was Rafelson's only chance. He reportedly spent the night with editor Morton Tubor and Screen Gems Vice President in charge of New Projects Steve Blauner (who would later partner with Rafelson and Schneider in their independent film company), creating quicker quick cuts to give the show a faster pace and by choosing to open the show with footage from the Jones' and Nesmith's screen tests to help familiarize the audience with the players. Then the network arranged a younger test audience and this newly edited version of the pilot received high enough ratings to gain a spot on the fall schedule. It did not hurt that Grant Tinker was among the young Screen Gems executives sitting in on the second cut. Blauner remembers that Tinker, the then assistant who would go on to become the producer of such 1970s hits as *The Mary Tyler Moore Show* and *The Bob Newhart Show* had an enthusiastic response: "I don't know what the hell I've seen but I think we should put it on the air." It became the biggest moneymaker in the history of Screen Gems due to the synergy (a word not yet invented) of the merchandising from record albums to comic books to lunch boxes to finger puppets. Tinker's instincts, which would do him well across his long producing career, were honed on *The Monkees*.

To achieve this amount of material to use in the editing bay, directors would have to manage 78 to 100 camera set ups a day, an unheard of number in an era when 30 set ups were considered a long day. They would also have to be free enough creatively to show the audience the metaphorical wizard behind the curtain, as did first-time director David Winters in "A Coffin Too Frequent" (written by Stella Linden). During a courtroom sequence Davy accuses "the barrister Dolenz" of a crime. In swinging over to Micky, the camera overshoots and focuses on Peter instead, though Micky can be heard off camera saying, "Over here." Peter whispers instructions to the director, "No, take it to Micky" while pointing at Micky who, when the camera swings back, can be found dancing in front of the camera to indicate where the camera should focus. Further farce came from using cockeyed or crooked camera angles, a technique popular on other sitcoms of the sixties. *The Monkees* employed this technique during the interrogation scenes of both "Monkees on a Wheel" and "Monkees Watch Their Feet." In several interviews both producer Rafelson and in-house director James Frawley discussed the need to hire young directors who would be willing to experiment and would not find such antics insulting to their typical working atmosphere.

As to the art of editing, *The Monkees* utilized the talents of three well-respected editors, lead by Mike Pozen who had won his Emmy in 1958 for *Gunsmoke* and gained another nomination in 1963 for *Ben Casey*. Gerald Shepherd had edited *Mister Ed,* and *The Addams Family* but would go on to edit *Five Easy Pieces* for Schneider and Rafelson) and Stanley Frazen came to *The Monkees* from *The George Burns and Gracie Allen Show*, quite the perfect preparation for breaking the fourth wall as the signature moment on *Burns and Allen* involved Burns narrating Allen's antics for the audience. Working together with the writers and directors the editors essentially explained editing to the audience with their antics. For a simple example, "Monkees on the Wheel," written by Coslough Johnson, directed by editor Gerald Shepard (one of the two he directed for the show) and edited by Pozen, involves a moment where the band members describe Peter's alias as having a white-collar criminal past. When they say he did two years in solitary confinement "standing on his head," the scene cuts to an upside down shot of Mike, not Peter. Later, as Peter is getting the real gangsters drunk, they cut to a shot of the other three Monkees on the couch saying in unison, "Isn't that dumb?" to the camera. The lines come from the writers and the quick cuts come from the editors. In "Wild Monkees" (written by Stanley Ralph Ross and directed by Jon C. Anderson and edited by Pozen) Peter gets water from the car for a coughing Mike. Instead, Mike drinks it and goes into an edited dance of crazy quick cuts while coughing up the water. The writers explain the behavior when it turns out Peter fetched the water from the car, he fetched it "from the radiator" to be exact. Then Davy responds, "It's a good job he didn't get it from the petrol tank."

In "Monstrous Monkee Mash" (written by Neil Nephew and David Panich, directed by James Frawley and edited by Pozen) when a frightened Micky piles chairs before the door to avoid the Wolfman, the film is sped up to highlight his fear and sense of panic. The creative team on *The Monkees* often used the frenetic personality of Micky's character in this fashion as in "Alias Micky Dolenz" (edited by Stanley Frazen).[2] In this episode Micky returns to the police station after being shot at by gangsters who think he is his look-alike, Baby Face Morales. Rather than use dialogue for Micky to explain what just happened (since the audience saw it happen) Bruce Kessler had the camera speed up to see Micky mimic the drive by to each cop in the room and run around in fear for a moment before settling into a chair where the camera returns to normal speed and Micky offers to help the police by impersonating Baby Face.

Another editing trick frequently employed on *The Monkees* involved inserting old movie footage to highlight lines of dialogue. Producers employ this technique for a few reasons, one of which is budget. Every few minutes you fill with footage already owned by the studio is a few more minutes you don't need to pay for new footage to be created. Secondly, this technique allows the writers and producers to offer the audience a look inside the character's mind, again making the audience feel even more intimately connected to their favorite characters. It is a technique usually reserved for comedies and so was open and frequently utilized on *The Monkees*. Examples include "Monkee Mayor" (written by Jack Winter, directed by Alex Singer and edited by Bernard Balmuth, for whom *The Monkees* served as his first professional job). When the band members find a slew of campaign contributions in their mail, Micky declares they will be able to "blow this town wide open" and the scene cuts to old demolition footage of a skyscraper exploding. Then Mike says it's too late to do so. After Micky answers, "We can blow this town wide closed!" the editor cuts to the same footage running backward and essentially rebuilding the old building. In "The Picture Frame" (written by Jack Winter, directed by James Frawley and edited by Mike Pozen) when a police officer comes to arrest them for the earlier bank robbery (in which they thought they were performing in a film) he begins shooting off his Tommy gun, causing damage to their pad. As the Tommy gun continues to fire, the film cuts to various damage moments in old films from a biplane crashing on the runway to old Model T's careening off the cliff into a lake.

New material could also be edited in to provide more of the fast pace desired by the creators. In "Too Many Girls" (written by Dave Evans, Gerald Gardner and Dee Caruso and edited by Gerald Shepard) random shots of women start popping up all over the band members' apartment, distracting Davy from rehearsing "(I'm Not Your) Stepping Stone." Likewise in "Success Story" (written by Bernie Orenstein, Gerald Gardner and Dee Caruso and edited by Stanley Frazen) when Davy admits he's "so hungry I could eat a horse," a shot of the boys wrangling a horse is edited in between shots of Davy. In "Monkee Chow Mein" (edited by Mike Pozen) when Peter and Micky are given the choice of four doors, one leading to freedom, they peek between each and find old film footage of a Sea Serpent, a wild west fight, and an exploding canon.

Finally, new material in the form of outtakes included in the course of an episode or added to the end in the form of a tag, often became inter-jected inside the locked script. These outtakes truly let the audience feel as if they were a part of the whole production, in on the laugh as it were. In the end that is one key to the success of the program, letting the young audience be a part of something at a time they felt they had little say in anything going on around them. For instance, "Monkee Chow Mein" included a moment where the Dragonman's yelling in Chinese quickly turned to English. When the actor, Joey Forman, catches himself speaking English, Micky responds, "Nice try, Dragonman. Want to try that again?" All of this remained in the final, aired episode. Similarly, in the teaser of "Monkees Blow Their Minds" (edited by Pozen) guest star Frank Zappa appears costumed as Mike and Mike costumed as Zappa. They hold an improvisational interview while Mike's fake Zappa nose keeps falling off. Zappa responds with phrases such as, "They have a lot of zany stuff on this program, huh kids?" and "This is one of our cute numbers for the show." Zappa speaks directly to the camera operator and to the audience when he says, "You see the way we worked this out in advance?" Later, referencing the use of cue cards, he asks, "Have you ever tried reading Mike and Frank?" In the midst of their fake interview they mention the piano and the director cuts to a shot of them at the piano where Zappa as Mike says, "Match cut–Here we go. We turn over and we all take our positions in front of the camera because this is the Monkees and we're really tricky."

Finally, "The Monkees Paw" (edited by Stanley Crawford) is a par-ticular favorite among shows that included outtakes, partially because it included so many in one show and partially because they were such raw looks at life inside the filming of a *Monkees* episode. The first outtake hap-pens while the band members all stand around a wooden Indian that dec-orates their pad. A curse has lead Micky to lose his voice, which means they will all lose a paying gig unless they can solve the problem. When Mike announces, "All we do is teach him to talk," Davy says, "How" with his hand raised up to match the pose of the wooden Indian and breaks up laughing, as do Mike and Peter who even covers his eyes in shock at the lameness of the joke. Later, as an insider joke, they use the song "Words" for the weekly romp which makes a fun in-joke since the episode deals with Micky losing his words. Then the episode ends with Mike saying "Well that wraps up another hilarious 30 minute episode. This is Mike Nesmith." Davy replies that he's Peter Tork, Micky claims to be Davy, and

Peter says he's Micky Dolenz and they break into an a cappella rendition of their theme song. Immediately after this impromptu goodbye the editor cuts to an outtake in Mendrake's (played by Hans Conreid) office with the lead actors goofing off rather than taking their places for the shot. As mentioned in Chapter Two, Conreid blurts out, "I hate these kids."

As an extra bonus this episode also contained one of the 19 end-of-show interviews that gave the viewers a chance to see the stars discussing their personal lives at a time before *Entertainment Tonight* or TMZ or any of the plethora of late night talk shows of the current era. While these interviews began ostensibly as a way to fill in a final minute or two if an episode ran short, they became signatures of the show which fostered respect for the actor/musicians and brought them closer to the audience. Rafelson found those final moments to be so important he left them raw. "Those interviews are strictly unedited. I don't touch them. I don't want to. If I have to edit them, out they go. I can tell you damn well they're not puppets, they're sensitive and intelligent–they have opinions on everything–they can speak for themselves."[3] These end-of-show interviews discussed everything from Davy's vist back home to England to the Sunset Strip riots and how they dealt with the incessant an untrue rumor that they could not play their own instruments.

One of the most obvious ways the program admitted to its audience that it was a program came when the actors often brought various behind the camera craft people in front of the camera as they did with property man Jack Williams on more than one occasion. This happened most often in the second season, most notably in episode 55, "Monkees Mind Their Manor," (written by Coslough Johnson). In a scene at the Customs Office, Davy is en route to England and trying to smuggle his bandmates onto the plane for free by hiding them in mummy cases. The actor playing the Customs Officer starts to tell Davy what wonderful lamps can be made from mummy cases when Davy interrupts, saying, "Don't think you're fooling us guys. We know who you are. You're Jack Williams, the property manager." Williams says, "Look, Sweetie, I may be Jack Williams, the property manager to you, but to 20 million teenagers I'm the Customs man." Davy steps to the camera to say, "You know, he really is Jack Williams." Then the camera focuses in on Jack who does an impression of Dean Martin as he liked to end *The Dean Martin Show*, which ran on NBC from 1965 to 1974. Williams said, "Upon closing folks, I want to thank Aunt Pat for sending in those peach preserves. Keep those cards and letters coming."

Then Williams goes into a rendition of Martin's ending song, "Everybody Loves Somebody," with Micky making faces behind him. The sound effects of teenage girls screaming at a Monkees concert are heard and Micky paws Williams like a fawning teenager at one of the many of the recent Monkees concerts.

On a side note, there are many connections between *The Dean Martin Show* and *The Monkees*, beginning with the connection between his daughter, Deana Martin, and The Monkees. She guest starred in "Some Like It Lukewarm" which aired as the next episode after "Mind Their Manor." Martin also had a connection to *The Monkees* via The Beatles and the song "Everybody Loves Somebody," which Martin had recorded several times in his career. But in 1964, when his 14-year-old son Dino, along with the rest of western civilization, adored The Beatles, Martin rereleased the song. He promised his son that it would knock "A Hard Day's Night" off its number one position on the Billboard charts where it had spent the last two weeks. Martin's song won the challenge. So when Jack Williams sang Martin's song he was both giving homage to another NBC property and winking at the competition between pop standards and rock 'n' roll. *The Monkees* had in fact made a visual reference to Dean Martin in the first season episode, "I've Got a Little Song Here" (written by Treva Silverman, directed by Bruce Kessler). When the band goes to Mammoth Studios to fool the fake music publisher into giving Mike his money back by having Micky pretend to be famous film mogul, they park in a spot reserved for Dean Martin. Dean Martin also had a stylistic connection to *The Monkees* via the metatextuality in his own show. Martin made no bones about the fact that he was working when he recorded his variety show. He admitted to reading off his cue cards and allowed any flubs to be included in the broadcast rather than do retakes. Finally, the 1966 summer replacement show which kept *The Dean Martin Show* timeslot warm was *Laugh-In*, which proved so successful it earned a spot in the regular season. *Laugh-In* became home to *Monkees* free-lance writer Coslough Johnson, who won an Emmy for his work there (and who happened to be the brother of *Laugh-In* cast member Arte Johnson). In the pre-production period of what would have been the third season of *The Monkees,* the actors discussed plans to create a more open variety-style show à la *Laugh-In*, but that season was not greenlit.

Rumors abounded that some of the older craft people (and some character actor guest stars) deeply disliked the unpredictability of working on set of *The Monkees* so finding one who was willing to go along with the joke might have been refreshing. Jack Williams must have been well loved by the actors on *The Monkees* because in episode 50, "Monstrous Monkee Mash" (written by Neil Nephew and David Panich) Davy calls for Jack when he and Micky find themselves transformed into a vampire and a werewolf. The characters are attempting to explain to guest vampire, played by Ron Masak, that they were in a fantasy sequence. Davy says, "We're the Monkees. You see in every show we do a fantasy sequence where we romp around and jump and do funny things and nobody interrupts us. Nobody." The Vampire acknowledges that they are all involved in a television show when he responds, "Well, it seems this show is different." Micky becomes defensive, "I'm warning you. Get out of our fantasy scene" and the Vampire challenges them with the question, "In these fantasies you say you can do whatever you want. Is that so? Then perhaps you try to take off your monster make up." When this proves impossible, Davy and Micky call for Jack Williams, but this time he does not appear. They then call "Cut" and the camera pulls back to find Masak sitting in a director's chair behind a camera saying, "No, no, my friends this is not fantasy—this is reality" as the story continues.

The program had begun its love affair with the properties department from the pilot. As mentioned previously, writer Treva Silverman said that for the musical romps the writers were asked to indicate props and sets and specify a few bits but let the actors and the director improvise the rest. This made the prop department the third improvisational collaborator. In the pilot, the writers experimented with giving Mike the nickname "Wool Hat" since he had sported one during his audition and he kept that look during filming. So later in the first season, in "Monkee Mayor" (written by freelancer Jack Winter) his bandmates choose Mike to run for mayor because, as Micky says, "You're the only one with a hat to throw in the ring." Then Mike asks where his hat is. An offstage prop man promptly tosses the hat in to him. Micky asks, "Where did you get that?" and Mike responds, "From wardrobe." This is actually a misnomer as the general rule of which craft department is responsible for which items splits hairs when it comes to clothing. If they are wearing a certain piece of clothing in a scene (à la the infamous wool hat) then it is a costume. If they are carrying it (such as in a pile they are cleaning off the floor—or by having it tossed to them) it becomes a prop. Late in season two props were still high on the list of laughable tools when in the tag of

"Monstrous Monkee Mash" (written by Neil Nephew and David Panich) a spell book seemingly floats in the air. A frightened Peter believes the Invisible Man has appeared, but Micky (again the actor raised on a television set) reassures him, "That's not the invisible man. That's special effects. That's wires holding the book up. Tinsel and fabric." Then they all take turns snipping the wires until Peter snips the last one and the book falls on his foot.

Sound is an art unto itself and, considering the program involved a group of young men making music for a living (or often not for a living), sound played a major role in the show. Aside from presenting the various musical moments in each episode, the innovative sound decision made by the producers and the actors came in the second season, when they officially dropped the laugh track, a recorded track of laughter made during radio days to recreate the atmosphere of live performances inside radio and, later, television production studios. Even after live audiences could be included in recording sessions of shows such as *I Love Lucy* these laugh tracks helped balance out the inconsistency of human laughter. Sound engineer Charles Douglass invented the art of 'sweetening' where the sound engineer raises or fades the volume on the recorded laughter to help the audience understand when to laugh in their living rooms. Sweetening also allows the sound engineer to act as the live audience by inserting laugh tracks on programs with no live audience. This usually occurs on multi-camera shows such as "*M*A*S*H*," filmed outside a studio, where a live audience would be impossible, so they had laugh tracks added to them. Networks had experimented with showing comedies such as *Hogan's Heroes* minus laugh tracks to test audiences who never seemed to know when to laugh and thereby gave the programs low scores.

During the second season of *The Monkees*, after "A Coffin Too Frequent," the actors requested the laugh track be eliminated because they felt since their younger, hipper audience had grown up with television, they were in fact the first generation to do so, they were indoctrinated into the style and understood when to laugh. Therefore the use of overly loud laughter when Davy is at the reading of a will in "Monkees Mind Their Manor" is an inside joke to the crew and the savvier members of the audience. Sadly, whether true or not, the NBC executives used this elimination of the laugh track as yet another excuse to cancel the show after the second season, claiming that it contributed to lower ratings.[4]

Against the backdrop of all this vivid sound, the visuals served as just as important a piece of the *Monkees* puzzle. The use of newer, bolder colors in costuming and set design helped create the visual riot that accompanied the verbal one. Dolenz biographer Mark Vigo believed, "The look of the show. The colors, the clothes and the weird musical numbers that were interspersed all had something to do with the appeal."[5] Gene Ashman served as costume supervisor. Ashman had worked on *Circus Boy* and was on *Bewitched* when asked about working on *The Monkees*. He worked so well with the creative team they brought him onto the film *Head* later. During his initial interview with producer Bert Schneider, Ashman was asked how he felt about young people. Focusing on the rapidly changing clothing styles he said, "The kids of today are very interesting and exciting and, clothes-wise, are into something quite different from anything that has ever been done before." He interviewed each of the cast members to help create the look of the show and agreed that while there would be a sense of uniform style to the clothes, they would then be customized to the tastes of each individual actor. For instance, his western background made Ashman design ten-inch side vents on all Nesmith's jackets while Dolenz would sport a more casual, double-breasted roller collar cut. Ashman gave Tork a form-fitting look to help him play different instruments with ease and the jackets he designed for Jones always had an English flare. Such looks were not easy to find at the time so Ashman traveled to San Francisco, imagining he would find a hipper look there. When that trip failed and he returned to Warner Brothers studio he accidentally wandered into a new men's shop called Lenny's Boot Parlor, owned by Lenny Able. Together they found, designed or supervised all the customized clothing for the characters, including individual shoes and matching boots.[6]

Keeping them all individual as opposed to forcing them into matching uniforms à la Paul Revere and the Raiders helped the audience distinguish them and possibly helped the band members manage their own personalities on the show and in concert. In the second season the actors began wearing their own clothing with a hippie flare or having such clothing designed for them. Dolenz remarks often in concert that the psychedelic poncho he wore while recording "Randy Scouse Git" was a tablecloth he had purchased in Mexico and asked his wife to alter into a poncho. How true that is is hard to say, but it does reference the idea that the actors influenced costumes in the second season. They were often seen in public and on concert tour in clothing that matched what appeared on the show, adding to their authenticity as real teenagers of their era. Together with Ashman's clothes, these styles proved so popular that teens around the world began sporting similar styles and annual Halloween costumes would be designed in the style as well.

The second question regarding the explosion of color created in the show's costumes is how was this accomplished in an era when less than half the audience owned color television sets? According to director of photography (DP) Dick Rawlings, whose credits range from *Charlie's Angels* to *Gilmore Girls* to *Desperate Housewives*, a combination of green and yellow Ratton filters were used by DPs to negate the color and judge the gray-scale contrast level.[7] When shooting in color the colors themselves provide depth, definition and contrast, but B&W photography is much harder because the depth and definition has to be created by more careful lighting to assure adequate contrast.

After costumes, the design and color of the set was handled by a set design team that included Ross Bellah, who had been nominated for an Oscar for in 1956 *Solid Gold Cadillac,* Phillip Bennett, who came off of *Dennis the Menace* and would go on to such '60s and '70s mainstays as *I Dream of Jeannie, Alias Smith and Jones* and *The Streets of San Francisco* before working on the Oscar-winning film *Ordinary People.* They were joined by set decorator Alfred E. Spencer, who began his career in films in the mid-1940s, worked with Judy Garland on *Summer Stock* in 1950 and moved into television with the *The Loretta Young Show.* After three episodes of *Circus Boy* and *77 Sunset Strip* and a season on *I Dream of Jeannie,* Spencer landed on *The Monkees.* Together they designed the Monkees' pad, stuffed to the rafters (literally) with posters and black and white headshots of Humphrey Bogart, assorted props that included the oft mentioned dummy, Mr. Schneider, the full size cigar store Indian statue and the spiral staircase which all allowed for free-wheeling improvisation, sometimes scripted, sometimes not. The apartment was designed with a practice area set in front of a large bay window looking onto the ocean to keep alive in many shots the idea that they (unexplainably) lived at the beach. They certainly had a collection of clearly yard sale castaway furniture, which made sense for a struggling band. The hand-embroidered wall hanging that announced "Money is the Root of all Evil" played a prominent role in many close ups. Beads were strung in the downstairs bedroom in a style that would not be repeated until Rhoda appeared in the pilot of *The Mary Tyler Moore Show.* The number four appeared frequently, for fun or to fuel the idea that they were a foursome. There was an eye chart on one wall and a bus schedule blackboard on another. Other random signs included "No Smoking or Street Clothes Beyond this Point" posted beside the door to the downstairs bedroom and "In Case of Emergency—Run!" posted beside the fire extinguisher hung on the wall.

Whether one credits the producers or each of these individual craft persons or a combination thereof with influencing the unique and timely aesthetic that surrounded the Monkees, it certainly stayed in the minds of the audience across the decades, and spawned new media across the years. According to Russ Kasmierczak, writing for the Nerdvana website in 2014, "Coupling slapstick and quip-riddled video with the trendiest music of the day, edited at a jackhammer's pace to accommodate a teenager's split second attention span, all in a mad attempt to grasp celebrity— thirty years ago, we called it MTV. Today we call it YouTube. I call it any episode of *The Monkees*."[8]

Eight

Theme(s) from The Monkees
Narrative Structure and Themes

Narrative structure is the combined study of the content, the theme, and the form or genre used to tell a story. Most television shows, movies and novels can be defined by one genre. They are westerns or they are science-fiction stories or they are romances. Rarely are too many genres included in one piece. For instance, one of the things that makes the musical *Joseph and the Amazing Technicolor Dreamcoat* unique is the way composers Tim Rice and Andrew Lloyd Webber chose to include a blend of song styles, from French ballads to Calypso to Klezmer, in the construction of the songbook. This keeps an audience continuously surprised and refreshed and made the musical both popular and educational to audiences across the decades. In a similar way, *The Monkees* kept its audiences guessing by varying the narrative style each week in a way few other programs were ever able to swap genres on such a regular basis. *Star Trek: The Next Generation* could sometimes tell stories in the western genre or the private eye genre through use of the holodeck but that is a rare opportunity. *The Mary Tyler Moore Show* never told a story in the science-fiction genre, nor did *Bonanza*. But *The Monkees* used many genres across 58 episodes. One of the few uniting factors to any episode was the way *The Monkees* brought vaudeville into the modern day, keeping it alive and passing the baton, as it were, to future shows aimed at the youth market such as *iCarly* and *Girl Meets World*.

Due to the way former cast members have defined the stories on *The Monkees* during countless interviews, casual viewers assume the genre of every episode was light romance. Dolenz, Nesmith and Tork often recall the show as merely a weekly romp around the trouble caused by plots involving Davy-wanting-a-woman/Davy-getting-a-woman or Davy-losing-a-woman. Many grown women who were once girls with crushes on Davy remember also those episodes best, likely because those episodes were among their most favorite reruns. When Jones guest starred on *The Brady Bunch* he did so as the long sought after crush of lead daughter, Marcia Brady, cementing the idea that this imitated a normal episode of *The Monkees*. In truth of the 58 episodes produced, only eight were rom-coms revolving around Davy's romantic misadventures. One episode, "Peter and the Debutante," made Tork the object of a rich young woman's affections and "Monkees Get Out More Dirt" involved Julie Newmar's character being in love with all four main characters at the same time to the detriment of her health. Many of those rom-coms were hybrids, blending other narrative styles within one episode.

The no-holds-barred improvisational aura of *The Monkees* espoused and enjoyed by the directors and the actors began with the writers. Most television sitcoms choose one structure and stick with it, with light comedy such as on *The Andy Griffith Show* being most popular before *The Monkees*. The *I Love Lucy* show made vaudevillian slapstick comedy its signature because of how masterfully Lucille Ball managed to mug. *Get Smart* (where *Monkees'* head writers Gerald Gardner and Dee Caruso once worked) stayed in the spy-parody genre for its entire run, never offering a western or science-fiction themed episode. By using a variety of narrative structures, *The Monkees'* innovation in narrative style helped the show stand out in its first season. Audiences learned to expect the unexpected, wrapped in what started out as seemingly familiar stories. These changing narrative structures became the signature of *The Monkees*, likely leading to its Emmy for Outstanding Comedy Series and might be the reason the deeper messages conveyed concerning hippie culture and the war in Vietnam could be so easily slipped into so many stories.

The mash up of reconfigured classics and audacious comedy might not alone have been enough to make the show so timeless. An overriding theme cinched the deal. According to Dolenz, who learned to understand the show from wearing all three hats: as an actor, a writer, and a director later in his career, "I used to talk about this in England to symposiums and work shops, talk about why it was so successful. I've been brought in many times by a production company that wants to do the 'new' Monkees but they cast it with all perfect looking people—I would never make that kind of cast—and in addition the band would already be successful or gain success quickly. In retrospect the very important theme of the show, part of the bible, is that The Monkees were never successful on the show. The Monkees were *struggling* to get success—that's what endeared us to all the kids around the world who were in their garages trying to be successful."[1] The overriding theme of struggling toward a dream did permeate most episodes no matter what other minor themes were being explored. This struggling band theme was appropriate for an era burgeoning with the kinds of garage bands that Gerry Goffin memorialized in the lyrics to "Pleasant Valley Sunday." Also, as noted by Tork and others, the absence of an adult living with the band members and micromanaging their career stood out to their teen and pre-teen audiences. Minor recurring themes would include the loftiness of creating music; the importance of friendship; watching out for the little guy and being loved for who you are.

The majority of *Monkees* stories utilized a potpourri of narrative structures including everything from surrealistic parodies based on classic films or novels to straight documentaries to spy thrillers to straight sitcoms. The only thing the writers never created was a straight drama, though "Success Story," where Davy thought he would have to leave the band, return to England with his grandfather, and never see his friends again, came close to a dramatic narrative. In fact, after Jones died, most news outlets played the clip from that episode that involved his saying goodbye to his American bandmates. Likewise, "The Devil and Peter Tork" offers evidence of the frequent use of parody, which follows the classic concept of taking known stories and clowning them up. The two documentary episodes consisted of footage taken during the band's early touring days presented as a special gift of thanks to their loyal television audience, who might not have been able to attend a live show.

If viewers saw only the ten or so light comedy style episodes, *The Monkees* looks much like the precursor to *The Big Bang Theory* as those episodes center around the friendship of four young adult males learning to live and love in a changing relationship landscape while pursuing their dream careers. In each show main characters both work and live together, something not normal in classic workplace comedies such as *The Mary Tyler Moore Show* or *30 Rock*. This makes *The Monkees* one of the first modern sitcoms to turn friends into family, meaning they were not the Pre-Fab Four but the Pre-fam four. By focusing on a family of friends,

The Monkees became a precursor to *Friends* in the '90s. Previous to *The Monkees* most comedies concerned sets of married couples who were friends and neighbors, reflecting then common American neighborhood patterns. For example, Lucy and Ricky Ricardo lived upstairs from Ethel and Fred Mertz. George Burns and Gracie Allen lived next door to Blanche and Harry Morton. Ralph and Alice Kramden lived in the apartment above Ed and Trixie Norton, etc. While breaking new ground for the portrayal of teenagers on television, *The Monkees* also broke new ground in genre, blending workplace comedies with family sitcoms, something critics point to *The Mary Tyler Moore Show* as having created yet this became another way *The Monkees* reflected modern culture before Mary Richards took her job at WJM. *The Monkees*' generation was one of the first where young adults moved far away from parents and relatives for a reason not related to a war such as the Civil War or World War II. Young adults in the 1960s attended colleges or took job offers in far off states or moved for the sake of self-discovery, making the friends they found in those new locales as much if not more important than family in terms of emotional support on a daily basis.

While beautiful young women were often provided for Davy in many episodes, few storylines focused mainly on his pursuit of a particular female, and those that did hit all the plot points of proper rom-coms. There would be what modern television and film writing manuals have designated the 'cute meet,' followed by a series of obstacles that kept the couple apart, and a miscommunication that threatened their reuniting. Comic sidekicks on both sides would appear to help, but also often serve as the cause of the miscommunication. Since this was a comedy Davy and the woman-of-the-week eventually overcame it all, though since *The Monkees* aired in the era before even comedies chose serialized storylines (where Leonard and Penny or Sheldon and Amy Farrah-Fowler's relationships grow week by week on *Big Bang Theory*) none of the girlfriends ever appeared again, leaving Davy free to pursue another love interest in a later episode without looking like a womanizer. This pattern was set in both the pilot episode, "Here Come the Monkees" and the first episode aired, "Royal Flush" and was repeated in "Some Like It Lukewarm," "The Chaperone," "Hillbilly Honeymoon," and "Monkees in Mexico." Each story involved Davy "cute-meeting" a girl he would then hope to date, whether it be meeting Vanessa, when her father hired the band for her Sweet 16 party, saving Princess Bettina from drowning, or meeting a disguised

Daphne, the girls' band member forced to dress as a boy to enter a co-ed rock band contest. Each story also involved a series of obstacles, often in the form of grown-ups: Vanessa's father, Bettina's Uncle, Jerry the Contest Show Host. The other band members Micky, Peter and Mike form the core of comic sidekicks and were joined by bungling security guards, bodyguards and female band members. A crisis always occurred where one of the band members had to tell the truth to save the day and that moment would be followed by the genre's typical joyful resolution. In each case Davy "got" the woman, who as noted earlier was never seen again.

Many of these rom-com narratives also suit other categories of narratives. "The Chaperone" falls under parodies of classic stories as it can trace its influence to the play *Charley's Aunt*, once a staple of the college stage. In *Charley's Aunt*, written by Brandon Thomas and performed originally in 1892 in London at The Theatre Royal, Bury St. Edmunds, the girlfriends of two young Oxford students, Jack and Charley, are allowed to stay for lunch only if there is a chaperone present, for purposes of social propriety. A rich aunt, Donna Lucia, is expected so all is well until her trip is delayed. In order not to miss meeting with the girls, Jack and Charley convince their friend Babbs, an amateur actor, to dress as Donna Lucia. Hilarity and jealousy ensue as Babbs is able to accept kisses from the young ladies while dressed as a woman that he could never accept while dressed as a man. While originating in London, this story became an American classic when George Abbott and Frank Loesser turned it into the musical *Where's Charley?* starring Ray Bolger (the beloved Scarecrow from *The Wizard of Oz*) in the late 1940s. In "The Chaperone" it is Micky who must don the dress in order to provide proper protection to Leslie, the daughter of the overprotective Gen. Harley Vandenberg.

Dressing in drag figured prominently in another rom-com, "Some Like It Lukewarm" (written by freelancers Joel Kane and Stanley Z. Cherry). This time it was Davy's turn so that their band could compete in a co-ed rock band talent show. Naturally, while in drag Davy met another woman of his dreams who herself had been dressing as a male so her all girl band (predating The Bangles and The Go-Go's) could compete against The Monkees. In the end the bands combined to win the show together. "Lukewarm" parodies the 1959 film *Some Like It Hot* (written by Billy Wilder and I.A.L. Diamond), which itself was loosely based on the French film *Fanfares of Love* (1935). Both of these films and "Lukewarm" predate the 1982 debut of the ultimate film version of drag, *Tootsie* (written by Larry Gelbart and Murray Schisgal). So on top of including the benchmarks of a proper rom-com, these two episodes, "Chaperone" and "Lukewarm" also incorporated the elements of *Charley's Aunt* and its other farcical descendants. In each story a young man dresses as a woman. In each story an inconvenient man falls in love with the character dressed in drag, causing complications to the maintenance of the disguise. In each story when the disguise is discovered it threatens the original goal of the story, yet when the reason for the disguise is admitted, the honesty leads to the gaining of the goal.

The last time a character dressed in drag for the bulk of an episode it was Mike in the "Fairy Tale" episode (written by Peter Meyerson), which appeared midway through the second season. While the narrative involved the bare bones of a rom-com story that focused on Peter rather than Davy, this episode was mostly a full-on farce complete with cardboard sets, dime-store costumes and multiple metatextual moments. The only flat out farce ever attempted, "Fairy Tale" involved Mike in the challenging dual role of both Mike the cobbler and in drag as the Queen that Peter's character worships. As part of the farcical element of the episode, Davy later played Little Red Riding Hood and Gretl while Micky played Goldilocks. No other episode breaks the fourth wall nearly as much from the cardboard sets to the stumbling delivery of dialogue to the anachronistic props that keep popping up. In commentary given by Nesmith on release of the full series to DVD he mentions the difference in the narrative style of "Fairy Tale" compared to the rest of the show's run. He also notes the way this episode's visual style blended with the wacky look of the Saturday morning cartoons that eventually surrounded the show in syndication. The look also blended with the kind of kitschy sketch comedy that *Laugh-In* presented successfully in the seasons after *The Monkees* cancelation.

Another hybrid, which blended rom-com with classic parody, "Prince and the Paupers" (written by Gerald Gardner & Dee Caruso and Peter Meyerson) has Davy helping his doppelganger propose to the woman of his dreams. The title and the doppelganger are the only plot points of the original novel, written by Mark Twain in 1882 that find their way into this story. In Twain's original story it is Prince Edward, son of King Henry VIII, who has a pauper who is his visual match and many lessons are learned about justice and the inequities of England's class system. What Davy learns in *The Monkees* version is to do the right thing. The rest of this episode's story also borrows from *Cyrano de Bergerac*, the French play originally written by Edmond Rostand in 1897 involving a man unable to approach the woman he loves so he has a friend woo her instead. In the play Cyrano is shy due to his long, ugly nose. In "Prince and the Paupers" the young prince is merely deeply shy. Being American television there would be no characters who were not perfect looking on screen. Either way, Davy saves the day by proposing to the prince's beloved Wendy while the rest of the band outwits the evil villains. In many ways this episode also borrows elements from the previous *Monkees* episode, "Royal Flush" in that a young royal must do something before their 18th birthday or lose their right to ascend to the throne.

While not Molière, these parodies helped introduce younger audiences to farce in the same way *Young Frankenstein* would in 1974 and again when made into a musical in 2007. They also prove that parodies were the bread and butter genre of *The Monkees*. Over 30 stories based in this genre appeared across the two seasons, which makes sense considering head writers Gerald Gardner and Dee Caruso came from two of the most successful parodies of the 1960s, *Get Smart* (1965–1970), a parody of the James Bond movie franchise, and *That Was the Week That Was* (1964–1965), a precursor to *The Daily Show* and the "Weekend News Update" sketch from *Saturday Night Live*. On *Week That Was* the team shared Emmy nominations in 1964 and 1965 with such eminent parody writers as Buck Henry, Herbert Sargent, Gloria Steinem, Calvin Trillin, Saul Turteltaub, and future *Monkees* writer David Panich. Therefore Gardner and Caruso brought over 20 parody ideas to the writers room and were more open to such ideas when other writers pitched them.

Unlike *Get Smart* where the only genre they parodied was spy thriller, on *The Monkees* the writers were free to parody them all, again keeping the audience guessing. Across the run of the show they would parody Hollywood films, gangster movies, monster movies, racing films, motorcycle sagas and a slew of other styles. This began with the second episode aired, "Monkee See, Monkee Die" (written by Treva Silverman) which involved all the clichés of the haunted house horror genre including the dilapidated old house, the foggy island (à la Agatha Christie's *Ten Little Indians*), the suspicious butler, the spiritualist, and the reading of the will of an eccentric millionaire. Being a *Monkees* episode there is also a pretty young girl in need of help who is eventually assisted by Davy and the gang. Elements of the horror genre include evil forces invading the everyday world, threatening the accepted social order and challenging the main characters both mentally and physically and appeared in several further episodes including "Monstrous Monkee Mash," "Monkee's Paw," "A Coffin too Frequent" and "I Was a Teenage Monster." In the latter the writers mixed elements of two legendary movie monsters, Frankenstein and the Werewolf, just a decade after Michael Landon, a teen idol on *Bonanza*, starred in *I Was a Teenage Wolfman* and two decades before Michael J. Fox would reprise the role in *Teen Wolf* (1985).

Considered a cousin to horror by some, the science-fiction genre is known for having both deeply attached fans and deep skeptics. It is also known for offering writers the chance to skirt censorship codes and comment on current societal conditions by placing those issues in the future and among aliens. Countless books, films and television shows, from *1984* to *Invasion of the Body Snatchers* to *Star Trek* used science-fiction for just such a purpose. Two of the *Monkees* episodes which parody science fiction also take the time to make pointed comments about then-current controversies in the United States. "Monkees Watch Their Feet" (written by Coslough Johnson) and "Frodis Caper/Mijacogeo" (written by Micky Dolenz and Dave Evans) each offered some of the deepest criticism of authority figures of any of the 58 episodes produced. Under the guise of dismissing and insulting the aliens, the various writers dismissed and insulted the cultural and political leaders of their day. Finally, "Watch Their Feet" also repeats the doppleganger element as the aliens create a robot that resembles Micky completely in order to infiltrate the human world.

As head writers, Gardner and Caruso had made sure all the other staff writers had approved stories and were off writing them before they tackled their first episode. As could be expected "The Spy Who Came In from the Cool" parodied spy thrillers. The title spoofed the 1963 film *The Spy Who Came In from the Cold*, which starred Richard Burton and was based on the novel by John Le Carré. In the *Monkees* episode Davy accidentally buys a pair of red maracas in which two Russian spies have hidden important microfilm. Gardner and Caruso invented the CIS, the Central Intelligence Service (instead of Agency), leftovers from their time writing for agents of CONTROL who were constantly battling KAOS on *Get Smart*. The writing team also borrowed from their *Get Smart* days in creating Dragonman, the evil Chinese villain of "Monkee Chow Mein." On *Get Smart* they had borrowed the Julius-No stereotype character from the

James Bond novel and film, *Dr. No*. For *The Monkees* they named him The Claw because of his prosthetic hand. Finally, they wrote another spy thriller, "Case of Missing Monkee," about Peter being abducted while searching for a kidnapped nuclear scientist he admired. Only one other writer, Treva Silverman (using the male pseudonym Lee Sanford), tackled a spy thriller. "The Card-Carrying Red Shoes" involved more secret microfilm, this time in the ballet slipper of a famous Druvanian (read Russian) female ballerina who falls in love with Peter (a pattern in Silverman's stories) for his beautiful face.

Gangster films are one of the writers' favorite genres to parody, enjoying giving Micky Dolenz a chance to do his Jimmy Cagney impression three times in the first season. This happened in "Monkees in a Ghost Town," which also parodied John Steinbeck's *Of Mice and Men*, and in "Monkees à la Carte," which was rife with Italian American clichés from meatballs to machine guns. Gangsters are the focus again in "Alias Micky Dolenz" which blends elements of "Prince and the Paupers" in terms of one of the Monkees having a double. This time the doppleganger is a match for Micky. In the final gangster parody, "Picture Frame/Bank Robbery," gangsters play a smaller role. Gangsters come in play when the crook, himself the parody of a movie producer, tells Micky, Mike and Davy that they have been hired to play bank robbers in a movie. In their interpretation bank robbers are cliché Italian gangsters. The bulk of the episode is more of a parody of police investigation scenes, Sherlock Holmes films and courtroom dramas. Likewise, "Monkees in a Ghost Town" served as a hybrid between gangsters and their cousin genre, westerns—a reminder of the way film theory often equates *The Godfather* with being a modern day western. Likewise, the first film produced by Bob Rafelson and Bert Schneider after *Head* was *Easy Rider*, nicknamed an acid western as it involved two motorcyclists traveling the American Southwest after selling cocaine.

The western genre was well served by *Monkees* storylines, possibly because of the ability to play off of Nesmith's natural accent. Granted, a traditional western needs to be a period piece, taking place between 1840 and 1900, something a *Monkees* episode could not create without a time travel device, which would take the story out of the western genre and into the science fiction/fantasy world. The other visual clue of a story being a western is the use of horses as a mode of transportation and this *could* happen and did happen in several episodes, particularly "Monkees in Texas" and "Don't Look a Gift Horse in the Mouth," written by Dave Evans particularly to highlight Jones' horsemanship. In "Hillbilly Honeymoon" the closest the story came to horses was the piles of hay in which Davy rolled with the generic young lady of the story. Other signals of a story being a western include stock characters such as the villain who threatens society, a hero who is willing to stand up as a protector, a good woman in love with the hero, and a bad woman in love with him, too. "Monkees in Texas" and "Hillbilly Honeymoon" landed squarely in the world of westerns with their reliance on such stock characters, on the locale of the American West, the use of a horse as a mode of transportation and the conflict between the individual and the community. "Hillbilly Honeymoon" and "Monkees in Texas" also prove metatextual in that they each parody a famous television program of the day. "Honeymoon" parodies the character of Ellie Mae Clampett from *The Beverly Hillbillies*, letting Ella Mae Chubber fall in love with Davy. Also, singer-songwriters Lester Flatt and Earl Scruggs, who wrote the theme song to *The Beverly Hillbillies* and often appeared on that program and its spinoffs, wrote much of the score to "Honeymoon," giving it both the look and the sound of the parent program. "Monkees in Texas" is a parody of the then ten-year-old fan favorite *Bonanza*, right down to naming the rancher and his three sons the Cartwheels rather than the Cartwrights. This inclusion of metatext allows the audience to be in on the joke. While "Don't Look a Gift Horse in the Mouth" brought the band to a farm to work, thereby including both the landscape and horse requirements of a western. Being set in the modern day it misses a major requirement of westerns, the time period.

After gangster and western genres, parodies of life as an entertainer dominated storylines whether it be the talent contests ("Your Friendly Neighborhood Kidnappers," "Too Many Girls" aka "Davy and Fern" and "Find the Monkees/The Audition"), the teen and style magazines ("Monkees à la Mode"), children's television ("Captain Crocodile"), teen films ("Monkees at the Movies") or a nod to Jones' earlier career on Broadway ("Monkees Manhattan Style"). The last few standalone parodies covered male-dominated genres such as the maritime adventures in "Monkees Marooned" and "Hitting the High Seas" and boxing films ("Monkees in the Ring").

Whether they were ahead of today's time with the rise of Marvel and D.C. Comics as powerhouses in film and television, or merely on par with it considering the popularity of *Batman* on television, *The Monkees* also dabbled in super hero adventures by creating the Monkeemen. Because shots of them in Monkeemen costumes appeared in the series' opening credits, it cemented the idea that the Monkeemen appeared more frequently than they did. Yet only three episodes involved Monkeemen: "I've Got a Little Song Here," "Monkee Chow Mein," and "I Was a 99 lb Weakling." They could most have used their super hero powers in the final episode, "Frodis Caper," and the evil villain's lair has a warning for "Monkees" approaching, but not for Monkeemen, and they do not appear in costume in this episode.

In the end the program functioned least often as a standard sitcom based on the antics of a group of friends or co-workers, but there were a handful of such shows, most often written by freelancers who came from other, regular sitcoms and did not realize they could push the envelope on *The Monkees*. "Monkee Mayor" (written by Jack Winter) put Mike in the running for mayor to aid a group of elderly neighbors. Neil Burstyn freelanced an episode where Micky needed to buff up to impress a woman, "I Was a 99 lb. Weakling," with writing credits that include Gardner and Caruso since as head writers they would have done the final polish on outside material. Burstyn also free-lanced the "The Monkees Christmas Show" episode with help from staff writer Dave Evans. That show served as a parody as well in that the band members take a Scrooge-like family and show them the beauty of being together at Christmas. "Success Story" was similarly polished by the head writers after being freelanced by Bernie Orenstein, who would go on to create *Sanford and Son*. As previously mentioned "Success Story" was part drama/part sitcom as it involves intricate vaudevillian planning to keep Davy's grandfather from first learning that he is not a success in America and then from making his plane on time.

It has often been said that *The Monkees* gave birth to MTV, which may or may not ever be provable. Certainly, the fact that each episode involved at least two musical montages showed that audiences enjoyed watching their favorite songs visualized and two episodes could be considered long videos à la Michael Jackson's *Thriller*, though those were more in the style of documentary. "Monkees On Tour" involved mini-interviews with each band member interwoven with footage taken from real concerts. The second documentary episode, "Monkees in Paris" is a half-hour romp through France with a music track but no dialogue or plot offered at all, except for the first five minutes of the show which are quite metatextual. Peter comes racing into the pad with a note about secret microfilm. The other actors give half-hearted reactions to the evil villain as he enters and director James Frawley enters frame to insist they do a better job. The actors break character to say they are tired of these repetitive storylines and are taking a vacation to Paris while the writers and producers prepare a better story. In discussing "Monkees On Tour" for the online *Headquarters Radio Show*, former associate producer Ward Sylvester identified that episode as "kind of outside our format unless you want to define *The Monkees* as having no format."[2]

The Monkees might never have planned to have no format but by doing so their chaotic narrative structure mirrored the freewheeling style shared by all the other creative artists contributing to the program. It kept the audience on their toes and kept them feeling fresh, despite the joke played in the opening of "The Monkees in Paris." It seems the actors did not recognize the value in the narrative variety the program offered as well as their audience did.

Nine

A Little Bit Me, a Little Bit You

Identity Construction and Confusion

The film-going audience generally expects actors to change characters from film to film, recognizing their actor personas as superceding their fictional characters and further recognizing those actors likely have quite different personas in their private lives. In television, however, due to the fact that the story plays out on a weekly basis across several years, often the fictional character supercedes the actor's persona in the mind of the audience. Often in television, the actor is hired to bring a particular, recognized persona to the program. Robert Wagner came to televison after working as an A player in a series of B films, often playing a suave, slightly bad boy, American-style ladies man. When he moved to television he played essentially the same type across three separate series: *It Takes a Thief* (1968–1970), *Switch* (1975–1978), and *Hart to Hart* (1979–1984). On the latter program, while still carrying the mantle of ladies man, he also portrayed a solidly happily married husband, capitalizing on the reputation he earned in real life with his second marriage to actress Natalie Wood. Likewise, Wagner's being cast as Tony Denozzo's father in *NCIS* in the 2010s played off his playboy past and highlighted the same aspects of the Denozzo character.

Now if the actors are less known when they appear on a television program and the characters deeply drawn, the program imprints that persona upon them, which can affect future casting decisions, often in a negative fashion. Henry Winkler *became* the Fonz and only the Fonz on *Happy Days* (1974–1984) for a long time; Tom Selleck *became Magnum P.I.* (1980–1988), making him hard to cast in other programs until *Blue Bloods* came

119

along over 20 years later and essentially offered the audience a future glimpse of Magnum; James Gandolfini *became* Tony Soprano, etc. Sometimes the imprint is entirely positive and creates a connection with the audience that they will follow through future work, such as the way Michael Landon's work as Little Joe Cartwright in *Bonanza* made him so beloved his audiences followed him into fatherhood on *Little House on the Prairie* and even into the afterlife on *Highway to Heaven.*

In this chapter the politics of identity construction will be understood through the process of examining the individual actors who became the Monkees. They will be examined for who they were coming into the production, who they became in the course of the production and how that influenced who they became afterwards. For instance, before being cast in the show, Dolenz identified professionally as an actor, not a drummer, but after the program ended the industry in which he had starred in two hit television shows identified him as a drummer, thwarting his opportunities for future casting. It could be said that when Dolenz broke into legitimate theatre on Broadway he was still being typecast as a former teen idol/Monkee since he played the '50s DJ Vince Fontaine in a revival of *Grease* from 1994 to 1998 and Zoser in Elton John's *Aida* from 2000 to 2004. Both roles involved an Elvis-like attitude often associated with rock and roll stars. This confusion over professional identifications hindered the further music career of Nesmith, who had trouble breaking the teen idol brand despite his track record of country-rock songwriting prowess and, of course, it trapped Jones in teen idol status as the Broadway musical world from which he sprang disrespected success in the television industry at that time. Yet when looking at the musicals of the 1970s in hindsight (*Hair, Godspell, Jesus Christ Superstar, 42nd Street*, etc.) one could imagine the matured Artful Dodger fitting in well. For Tork being typecast as naïve and childish interfered with his chances to be accepted afterwards in a mainstream rock and roll world that revolved around the mature, raw sexuality of a Jim Morrison. For Dolenz, Jones and Tork, their instant identification as friends who belonged together made casting them as guests on *Boy Meets World* for "Rave On" (season 3, episode 8) an easy decision.

In the case of *The Monkees,* identity confusion came from the start since they were not immediately recognized entities coming into the production *and* the choice was made to use their real names rather than fictional ones. Of the group of them, Dolenz had the greatest chance of being recognized by the television audience due to the two seasons he spent playing Corky on *Circus Boy* in the late 1950s. As an actor in that series, however, he had used the last name Braddock and his hair had been dyed blonde to avoid any connection to his actor father, George Dolenz (then starring in *The Count of Monte Cristo*). In a world minus *People Magazine*, *Entertainment Tonight* and celebrity websites, it is likely a majority of the audience did not make that connection between 10-year-old Micky Braddock and 20-year-old Micky Dolenz. For those who did, Dolenz brought the family-friendly atmosphere of *Circus Boy* to *The Monkees* at a time when long-haired teenagers weren't to be trusted on television. Likewise, Jones brought the benefit of a Broadway pedigree, one that is more recognized in today's uber connected world where audiences knew that Neil Patrick Harris was also a Broadway performer when they saw him on *How I Met Your Mother*. Since many members of *The Monkees* target audience watched *The Ed Sullivan Show* on February 9, 1964, to see The Beatles perform, they also saw the young Jones in his role as the Artful Dodger in *Oliver!* Having had no such mass media experience yet, Nesmith and Tork remained new to the television audience and open to the definitions the audience—and the writers—chose to assign them.

As to using their real names as the names of their characters, there was television precedent as this had been done with George Burns and Gracie Allen, Jack and Mary Benny and, most famously, Jerry Seinfeld, who played himself while the other characters around him played fictional versions of his friends on *Seinfeld*. During their 2013 reunion tour blogger Russ Kazmierczak, Jr., commented that "the line between the Monkees as actors and their zany onscreen personas was so blurred because they opted to use their real names throughout—a logical choice when establishing a franchised band, but rather short-sighted in retrospect if the guys had any hopes of shedding their Monkee skin later in life. Just ask Jerry Seinfeld, or any other comedic lead that used his real name in the role that defined his career. The trend had to start somewhere."[1] *The Monkees* rests rightfully in the center of all that identity confusion and might be most synonymous with Ozzie and Harriet Nelson and their own teenage singing sensation, son Ricky Nelson. Ricky Nelson went by his real name on his parents' program and like the Monkees, took that name into his rock and roll concert career. But *Ozzie and Harriet* further complicated the reality of *The Monkees* since the Nelsons actually were a family as well as playing one on TV, whereas the Monkees were not a family; the Monkees were not yet even a group of friends when they were cast in the show. Though the fictional Ricky Nelson was not the real one, the difference as far as the audience was concerned was minimal. The private Nelson was drawn to harder rock music, but his father's control of his career kept him from performing on music shows such as *Shindig* and kept him from recording too much hard rock, making the private persona of Nelson appear closer to the fictional Nelson. While that assumption proved detrimental to Nelson's future career, the same would happen to the various actors who portrayed the Monkees. Not only did they use their own names for the show's characters, they ended season one with an episode titled "The Monkees on Tour," a documentary about their first live concert tour involving interviews with each of them as well as onstage footage of each performing their individually chosen solo numbers. Likewise, several episodes ended with short, one or two-minute interview segments where they spoke of their own lives as performers quickly gaining fame, *not* as their fictional financial-failure-of-a-band characters. So who were these actors and how did exposure on the program affect who they would become?

Sociologists and social psychologists have long studied the way people construct their identity based on descriptors both in and out of their control such as sport or music preference (in) and gender and ethnicity (out). Identity is an ever-changing construct for most people. It is even more so for actors whose identity changes with the different parts they play and whose identity is a construction never completely under their own control. As has been shown, an actor's identity is often at the whims and needs of others interested in their own current financial success and future profit more than in that of the actor involved. In the case of the actors who were cast in *The Monkees*, these other interested parties included the producers, the network, the recording company, the teen magazines and the advertisers. Finally, due to their continued, successful revivals across the decades, VH1 produced a television film about the creation of the show in 2000. *Daydream Believers: The Monkees' Story*, gave writer Ron McGee the chance to add one more fictional layer to the persona of each actor.

The producers calculated each actor they cast, looking for characteristics they imagined would appeal to the particular group of fans they were hoping to engage. The casting process has been well documented in other books so a short history will suffice. It all began by posting an ad for an open casting call in *The Hollywood Reporter* on September 8, 1965. "Folk and Roll Musicians and Singers for acting roles in new TV series. Running parts for 4 insane boys, 17–21. Want spirited Ben Frank's types. Have courage to work. Must come down for interview. Call HO.6–5188." In an attempt to recreate the dynamics of The Beatles and the new generation of fans they engaged, the request to 'come down' for the interview has often been interpreted to mean the actors should not arrive high on any particular drugs. Each actor arrived in a different fashion with Jones and Dolenz being sent by managers and agents, Tork arriving on the recommendation of a friend, Stephen Stills, who did not land a part, and Nesmith coming to the open casting call. In *E! Hollywood True Story* casting director Eddie Foy III (himself a child of Hollywood) recalled, "They had a charisma and a magnetism that jumped off the screen and there was a freedom that drew the younger audience and they were also the audience that bought records." In effect, the group was engineered to do exactly what it eventually did, outselling The Beatles and Rolling Stones in album sales in 1968 while flooding the market with ancilliary merchandise from lunch boxes to finger puppets.

While the music was the marketing miracle, it was the program that created their personas. Rafelson remembered, "We interviewed several hundred guys. We didn't want professional actors–they're too concerned with image and acting technique. We finally settled on Peter, Mike, Micky, and one Englishman, Davy. They had not met before, they were all musicians. The one quality above all else was that they came over as original people."[2] Unpacking the phase "came over" reminds the reader of the quote variously attributed to George Burns, Groucho Marx and French diplomat Jean Giraudoux: "The most important thing is honesty. Once you can fake that, you've got it made." How could producers assume that what these (or any) actors presented in an audition 'came over' as their original selves? Aware of the audition process actors are always performing. Still, the personas the four actors provided appealed to the producers and resulted in their being cast. At that point, producers, writers and network executives would begin to carve the actors into characters based on what they believed the audience would most enjoy watching and supporting.

Each in his own right was an authentic, mostly American teenager from various parts of the world, Nesmith the too-young-married Texan, Tork the Connecticut gentleman, Dolenz the Cruise Night Valley boy, a character type later glamorized in *American Graffiti* (1973), and Jones who offered a throwback to the 19th century teenage life of apprenticeship, first to a racing stable and then to an agent. So they were all, before the show began, authentic teenagers of the 1960s and those personas became the foundation for their fictional selves, though soon authenticity trumped fiction. In the ITV documentary, *We Love the Monkees* (2012) set photographer Henry Dilz said, "By the second season they weren't playing a role anymore. They were being themselves. They started wearing more of what they felt comfortable in, like Micky wore the big poncho and they just wore what they would normally wear." According to an interview with *The Phoenix* in the wake of the show's cancellation, Nesmith gave his own definition of each group member: "Now we'll be able to do the things the way we want to. We each have our own style—Peter is understatement, quieter, melodic; Micky is ragtime, old-fashioned; Davy is Broadway, mohair tuxedo; and I'm hard-driven West Coast rock—and our albums will have a bit of each."[3]

In a 1989 interview with the online Headquarters Radio Show, associate producer Ward Sylvester recalled the search as looking for four disparate types, as being different than most groups forming at the time where all the members were similar. He described their search as focusing on looking for a Will Rogers kind of country and western figure; a Hunts Hall character (the actor who played Sach Jones in the Bowery Boys films in the 1940s and '50s) who seems very well-meaning but not quite with it. Peter Tork played that character. He was the only one acting and playing a character different from himself—a little bit of a dimwit, the attitude of that character wasn't that he was stupid but he was just kind of unsure of himself. Then they cast Dolenz in the Jerry Lewis kind of high energy type who had some kind of experience acting in front of a camera and they had Jones as their requisite teen idol. "Being English was very in for pop stars. We tried to balance the group for those roles. With the exception of Micky we decided to choose actors who were unschooled in the film medium with actors who were essentially being themselves or being open to improving all the time." As Sylvester remembered it, they wanted actors who could be spontaneous and still be themselves.[4] This returns us to the question, which selves were they being at which time?

In a 1968 *Tiger Beat* article on the changing style of Dolenz's hair, writer Ralph Benner noted what he thought made The Monkees special to his readers: "There was, however, a difference with the Monkees. When they were chosen, they were picked to fit into a vaguely sketched character as one member in a group of four. What is groovy about the conception of the Monkees is that each boy was picked for the remarkable individuality he would lend to his loosely written character."[5] According to Neil Cossar of This Day in Music, on the program, "Each of the four was given a different personality to portray: Dolenz the funny one, Nesmith the smart and serious one, Tork the naive one, and Jones the cute one. Their characters were loosely based on their real selves, with the exception of Tork, who was actually a quiet intellectual. The character types also had much in common with the respective personalities of The Beatles, with Dolenz representing the madcap attitude of John Lennon, Nesmith affecting the deadpan seriousness of George Harrison, Tork depicting the odd-man-out quality of Ringo Starr, and Jones conveying the pin-up appeal of Paul McCartney."[6] In the beginning they were based on both stock comedic characters, loosely matched to Beatles' members, yet some audience members remembered they differed from The Beatles in comforting ways. After Jones' death Daily Mail contributor Liz Jones (no relation) recalled, "While The Beatles became too miserable, too strange—I bought the Magical Mystery Tour EP, but found the lyrics to I Am The Walrus, with its mention of dead dogs, gave me nightmares—The Monkees, who outsold The Beatles in 1967, at the peak of their fame, were safe and wholesome."[7] Clearly, the impressions of the program were mixed even from the start. Some audience members—parents and children alike—saw *The Monkees* as subversive while some saw them as wholesome enough for Jones and Dolenz to eventually headline the Flower Power Concert Series at the Epcot Center at Walt Disney World in 2012 and 2013.

Defining each character as distinctly different from the others became one of the first jobs for the writing staff. It was an issue from beginning, when the pilot earned low scores in testing and was nearly scrapped with one complaint being audience members could not keep track of the characters. The solution became adding sections of the audition tapes for both Nesmith and Jones to the pilot, thus allowing the audience to see them as individuals. But certainly a good chunk of the first few episodes then revolved around pointing out each character's differences. This can be confusing considering episodes aired out of order to their filming, based on the network executives choosing the ones they thought best sold the series in its first months. So "Don't Look a Gift Horse in the Mouth" (written by Dave Evans), which defined Davy as a horseman, filmed first but aired 8th, perhaps because "Royal Flush" (by Peter Meyerson and Robert

Schlitt), which also focused on defining Davy, this time as an Englishman, filmed second but aired first after the pilot. Therefore, Davy's character did not immediately require further explanation, though it is noticeable that several early episodes focused on Davy, perhaps in the understanding that the key audience already knew him from the teen magazine build up he received. By episode four it was time to establish the four individuals as a coherent group. "Monkee See Monkee Die" (written by Treva Silverman) filmed fourth and aired fourth set up The Monkees as a poor but dedicated group (they are rehearsing in their pad when the landlord comes by threatening to evict them for late payment of rent) and when they go to the reading of the will at the haunted mansion, rather than see each member receive one remembrance from the dead millionaire, the whole group inherits his pipe organ. They even sleep in the same bed together.

This was followed by the episode that filmed and aired third—"Monkee vs Machine." Written by David Panich, it focused on defining Peter as unemployable outside of music and Mike as the fatherly figure of the foursome. The writers did not get around to focusing on Micky until he dressed in drag in "The Chaperone" (written by Gerald Gardner and Dee Caruso) which filmed 8th and aired 9th. Did they have more belief in his standing out due to his past television exposure, his being the comic relief or being more easily recognizable since he sat alone behind the drums? In fact, in the fifth episode of the first season, "The Spy Who Came In from the Cool," as writers Gardner and Caruso were still solidifying the characters to make them easier for the audience to understand, Dolenz is referred to merely as the drummer but is then shown engaging in both physical comedy and verbal banter. This episode involved the C.I.S. spying on the Monkees. The quick descriptions the agents gave of the fictional band members are clearly the things the writers wanted to solidify: Tork is called the quiet one and marked as a bit slow because when asked, "How do you feel about [political] demonstrations?" Peter responds, "They are the only way to sell a vacuum." Next Nesmith is called the leader and shown taking charge while Davy is defined merely as "the English boy," though he is also showcased as a ham as he tap dances to Stephen Foster's "Old Folks at Home" with a cane and straw hat when he knows he's being photographed.

Eventually, the band members' individual personalities were made apparent enough that they could even joke about the earlier confusion. In "Monkees Paw" (episode 51, season two) the show ends with Mike saying, "Well that wraps up another hilarious 30 minute episode. This is Mike Nesmith." Davy says he's Peter Tork, Micky says he's Davy Jones, and Peter says he's Micky Dolenz. At that point, after over a year of exposure in the teen magazines of the day, it could be assumed the audience knew them all individually enough to be in on the joke. Likewise, at the beginning of the second season the actors and producers shared the joke every week by weaving it into the opening credits. While they had added concert footage to the credits they had also added a bit where, starting with Davy, as his face came into close-up the name "Peter" appeared and Davy's face fell. Cut to a shot of a saddened Peter, followed by a shot of Davy with his proper first name appearing as he smiles. Repeat the beat with Micky, then Mike, who claps with joy at the appearance of his correct name, until finally Peter's face appears with his own name and he gently smiles. This gimmick proved another metatextual way of letting the audience in on the idea that this was a television program they were effectively helping to make through their particpation in the joke.

The other way fans participated in the identity creation of each character came in the way they enshrined each actor in public memory. While producers Rafelson and Schneider may have thought they cast what amounted to four parts of the perfect man—humor (Micky), heart (Davy), sweet natured (Peter) and smart (Mike), over time they became more properly recognized as the voice (Micky), the face (Davy), the craftsman/musician (Peter) and the prolific songwriter/entrepreneur (Mike).

The Voice—Micky

Identity construction can best be seen in the career of Micky Dolenz, who as noted earlier, came to the cast with another show already under his belt and came to the project as an actor via an audition rather than through a cattle call. Audiences recognized his parents as actors and some knew him as the former star of *Circus Boy*. In fact, early versions of the credits (which appeared as ending credits on the pilot rather than opening ones as would become the norm) had Dolenz identified as "Micky Braddock."[8] As noted in Chapter Six, the writers gave a nod to this history in "Monkees at the Circus" which opens with Micky saying "I haven't been to the circus since I was a kid." Then Micky sings the *Circus Boy* theme song.

In the course of the program and his work in the band Dolenz would become both a drummer and a songwriter ("Randy Scouse Git," "Mommy and Daddy," "Regional Girl"). Post the program's cancellation the actor part of Dolenz would confront typecasting in the continuation of his acting career on television. First he would only be offered roles such as the one on *My Three Sons* where he played a rich rock and roller, whose storyline tempted Chip to give up his college engineering studies to join a band. Eventually, Dolenz often notes in interviews, typecasting damaged his career such that he was not offered roles outside the realm of rock and roller. For example, he was not cast as Fonzie in *Happy Days* because his Monkee persona was still too powerful and would overwhelm the rest of the relatively unknown cast.[9] (Of note is the fact that *Happy Days* involved casting the teenaged Ron Howard who audiences remembered as Opie Taylor from *The Andy Griffith Show)*. When typecasting became apparent, Dolenz turned to the theatre in another country, England, and performed in *The Point* (written by Monkees songwriter Harry Nilsson). He also applied for and received a series of directing jobs. This move brought him behind the camera for nearly a decade. When he returned to the United States it was as a singer in the 20th anniversary reunion tours and then to the theatre rather than television (*Pippin, Aida, Hairspray!*) because Broadway audiences are comfortable with actors and actresses appearing again and again in a new guise. In 2014 he was cast to originate the lead role in *Comedy Is Hard!* by Mike Reiss. Since the play involves the rivalry between a retired stand-up comedian and a classical actress in a home for retired actors, it can be said to be typecasting Dolenz yet again.

As an actor, Dolenz understood the idea of creating a character and further, he understood that "Micky the Monkee" was and is a character. He referenced that in his uncut interview with MTV at the start of the 1986 first reunion tour. When they asked him to do a promo he asked, "As (myself) or as Micky the Monkee?" Also, in his singing performances, whether with the Davy, Peter, Micky combination or the Mike, Peter, Micky combination—or with David Cassidy and Peter Noone as the Ultimate Teen Idols—Dolenz appears with the hat that obscures the hair loss and reinforces the existence of "Micky the Monkee." Conversely, in his work on Broadway in *Hairspray!* he willingly appeared minus the hat, allowing his receding hairline to show because it suited the character of Wilbur Turnblad. In an interview connected to the 2014 summer reunion tour with Nesmith and Tork, Dolenz clarified his point about Micky being a character. "I was cast in that television show. And I was playing the wacky drummer, and singing the songs and playing the drums, and acting and improvising and playing the part on the television show. So when I revisit or am asked to go on tour, or whatever, I consider that I'm recreating that role for that period of time, to some degree—much in the same way that you would say—like I just mentioned that I just did 'Hairspray' in London and in England for almost a year. Well, I may not do that show again, but if I were to be asked, and I went back to do that show—I was playing Wilbur, the father in that show. And, you know, I would go back and be Wilbur again. So I'll always be associated with *The Monkees*, there's no question about that. But I'm not a Monkee every day [Laughs]."[10] In a similar vein, in discussing his cameo in Rob Zombie's 2007 remake of *Halloween* for the Something Else Blog, Dolenz said he was thrilled to learn that Zombie would be using him as a gun-shop owner rather than as a cameo of Micky the Monkee: "When I found out I wasn't playing myself, I got excited. I don't like playing myself. As it turned out, it's one of the best little pieces of footage I have that I've done."[11]

In terms of creating the fictional identity of "Micky the Monkee," Dolenz felt the writers created the character more so than he did: "They were looking for that guy who just jumped off the screen at them. And to say how much of it was me—I don't know if I can quantify it. They developed that character of the wacky drummer. They gave me the funny voice. I don't do funny voices all the time and I don't run backward at a high rate of speed. But it was partly my personality."[12] Something Dolenz did have input into was his becoming the de facto lead singer of both the fictional and real bands. Because his voice most suited the original music supervisor, Don Krishner, Dolenz was chosen to sing lead on the first single released, "Last Train to Clarksville" and on subsequent chart-topping songs, notably "I'm a Believer," while Jones took lead on most of the romantic ballads. Proof of Dolenz' status as lead singer came in "Monkee's Paw" (season two, episode 19). Though rock and roll drummers are rarely lead singers, this episode enshrined Micky as lead singer. Once he lost his voice to the curse of an old monkey's paw and the band is threatened with losing their current job, none of the others take his place. Instead, they spend the episode making desperate comedic attempts to undo the curse in order to keep the job.

The Face (and the Englishman)—Davy

Jones offers another version of identity construction, perhaps a tougher example of typecasting, one that he spoke of often in his later years. Jones was trapped in the role of Teen Idol before he was cast in *The Monkees*—an identity he eventually overwhelmed and which overwhelmed the rest of his career. On a *CBS Sunday Morning* interview he discussed his desire—and ability—to play the part of a 63-year-old, but the lack of interest producers and audiences had in seeing him as a grandfather. During their reunion tours, his stage patter involved taking the audience back to a time when, "I was that boy and you were that girl" or joking about all the girls—and boys—who dreamed of him, staring at his posters on their bedroom walls and even kissing those posters good night. So tied to either the Monkees or *Oliver!* was Jones that his most financially successful work later in life came from the reunion tours and from stage work in revivals of *Oliver!* where, as Fagin, he in essence played the grown up version of the Artful Dodger character that had earned him his Tony nomination.

Forced into the teen idol role by Hollywood Jones was the one teen idol that resonated across the years. Jones pondered what it meant to have posters of his face plastered across so many teenagers walls when he co-wrote the song "Ceiling in My Room" (with Dominick DeMieri and Robert Dick) for the group's fifth album *The Birds, The Bees and The Monkees*. In 2008 Yahoo! Music named him Top Teen Idol of All Time, ahead of Michael Jackson and David Cassidy, Bobby Sherman and Donny Osmond, all equally famous in the early 1970s. While Bobby Sherman and David Cassidy faded from view, Jones maintained his status. According to "Why We Grieve Teen Idols," written the day after his death in 2012: "Jones was someone younger generations looked up to as 'the first person who made them interested in music,' said Phil Gallo, Billboard's senior correspondent. But that fandom isn't limited to the girls who would have gladly traded a limb for a date with Jones. 'When I was a kid, I wanted to BE Davy Jones,' actor Kevin Bacon tweeted upon Jones' death. 'Big part of what led me to showbiz.'"[13]

A measure of Jones' standing also comes from considering the massive amount of international news outlets, from Australia to Japan that covered his death in 2012. The evening news on all three American broadcast channels covered the story, with Diane Sawyer announcing that a "startling bulletin came across in the newsroom." She then proclaimed "He is still that forever young and sunny singer from *The Monkees* who made more than one generation want to sing along." Why would a serious journalist (not merely an entertainment reporter) consider news of the death of a former teen idol 'startling' unless she, too, had once been among his fans? Later in the piece they identify "Getting Davy Jones," *The Brady Bunch* episode on which he guest starred, as the "single most re-run episode of television ever" and they back up Walter Koenig's story that his character on *Star Trek* was styled "like Davy Jones to appeal to younger viewers." Perhaps more startling was the coverage given by the artistic feature magazine *CBS Sunday Morning*, which usually focuses on the best of Broadway, ballet and other higher brow art forms, yet included a retrospective on Jones' life. Likewise, countless writers and performers dedicated columns to what Jones' death—and life—meant to them, from Penn Jillette to Mitch Albom to Richard Marx. Celebrities and average fans flooded the newest social media outlet, Twitter, with discussions of his loss.

Why is Jones, and not Sherman or Jackson or Cassidy, considered the greatest Teen Idol? It could be the existence of that *The Brady Bunch* episode, which enshrined him to the television audience as the ultimate teen idol. While other programs starring teen idols fell out of rerun favor, *The Brady Bunch* continued, which meant Jones kept showing up as Marcia's dream date over and over again. That constant reminder of his existence, even at times when *The Monkees* was not in rerun rotation, kept Jones an evergreen example of the classic teen idol. The writers of *The Brady Bunch Movie* (1995) considered that episode so iconic they included it in their film and included a cameo by Jones with the joke that modern students did not know who he was, but the female teachers all clustered around the stage screaming. Certainly the studio cultivated that character for him even before *The Monkees*, grooming him with guest starring roles as a singer on family-friendly programs such as *Ben Casey* and *The Farmer's Daughter* (where he sang a straight version of "Gonna Buy Me a Dog" before the comic duet with Micky that appeared on *The Monkees*.)

With the studio's previous backing, the writers followed their lead and focused on creating Davy's character highlighting his boyish good looks, his English accent, his smaller stature and his ability to be a song and dance man. The pilot focused on his being the leading man since the female guest character had the soon-to-be-cliché starry eyes only for him.

Women fell for him in the majority of episodes in each season with only one or two per season focusing on other characters functioning as the romantic lead ("One Man Shy" for Peter and "I Was a 99 lb. Weakling" for Micky). In episode fifteen of season one, aptly titled "Too Many Girls," writer Dave Evans spends the whole episode defining Davy as all of the previous points. It's obvious Davy is the teen idol/romantic lead since adoring girls keep popping up in the pad in the opening segment of the show. When Mike bemoans the fact that Davy is "trapped by his own staggering good looks," Micky responds, "I, myself, am deeply jealous." Early on, a guest character remarks on Davy's being English and lures him into her restaurant with an offer of tea. When he has his tea leaves read and they predict he's going to fall in love within the next 24 hours, Mike says, "He does that every day." Later, Davy says he knows why they are keeping him away from women, "It's 'cause I'm short." That phrase became embedded in the fans' minds through the patter the band chose to include at the opening of "Daydream Believer" on *The Birds, The Bees and The Monkees* album. (Davy: "What number is this, Jim?" Band: "7A," Davy: "Okay. I mean it. Don't get excited, man. It's 'cause I'm short.") Perhaps his stature made for his appeal because it kept him a safe dream lover. Certainly, the writers used it for visual gags, including the fantasy sequence in "Son of a Gypsy" where after he has been tortured on the rack he stands up and towers over his 6-foot-plus bandmates by a foot and a half.

Clearly, romance was the focus for his character. In "Prince and the Paupers" it is Davy who must woo the woman in the pseudo-Cyrano story of a shy prince who must marry or lose his kingdom. In "Monkees at the Movies" the fictional Davy takes on the role of real life teen idol when he takes over for the arrogant character played by Bobby Sherman, already an established teen idol from his two years on *Shindig* (1964–1966). (The year after Sherman's appearance he earned the role of Jeremy Bolt on *Here Come the Brides* and earned several gold records, which brought him to his fullest fame. In a further tie-in with Davy, Sherman toured with Jones and Peter Noone in the 1998 Teen Idol Tour.)

As to the focus on Jones' boyish face, "The Card Carrying Red Shoes" acknowledges Davy as the face of the group when Russian dancer Natasha threatens to shoot Micky and Davy but not Peter because she has fallen in love with his face. Davy points to his own face and says, "What is this, chopped liver?" and Peter responds, "Well, it can't be you every week, Davy." Perhaps not that week, but most often Davy's was the face. Over thirty years later, in the 2001 reunion concert tour, Micky called Davy "the face," explaining that in Greek mythology there was Helen of Troy, the face that launched a 1000 ships, and in Monkee mythology there was Davy Jones, the face that launched a 1000 lunch boxes. This serves as a reminder that the marketing campaign around *The Monkees* also contributed to making Jones the ultimate teen idol. So many fans 'owned' a visual piece of his character, from posters to finger puppets to paper dolls, they came to feel they owned him. Long after new episodes involving that character ceased to exist, Jones continued to exist in the most intimate space of their home—their bedroom. When asked what she dreams about, Tony Award winning composer and pop diva Cyndi Lauper told the *Daily Mail,* "What or who do you dream about? I have vivid dreams—from banal to crazy. One time I was married to Davy Jones of The Monkees. Go figure!"

This near worship of Davy caused a sometimes-crippling effect on Jones as his fans never equally embraced him in any other role. But that near worship also made his early death all the more catastrophic, creating a plethora of personal tributes across the internet when the news broke. No less a literary expert on death, author Mitch Albom (*Tuesdays with Morrie, The Five People You Meet in Heaven*) began his tribute column with, "Davy Jones died. I didn't think that was possible. If there was ever a forever-young pop idol, Davy was it. Boyish-faced, long-haired, short, thin, British accent, always goofing around with the other Monkees." Albom explained Jones' appeal as personifying "a time when being a teen idol was a huge business, but still a relatively innocent one."[14] That innocence so stuck to Jones' post–Monkee persona that he was invited by beloved children's author Sandra Boynton to record music for the audio version of her *My Personal Penguin* and her collection of jukebox-inspired songs, *Blue Moo.* Albom also believes the lesser exposure Jones received, as opposed to the 24/7 TMZ world of performers in the early 21st century, contributed to his appeal but in the end admits, "I don't know why his passing saddens me as much as it does…. Maybe it's just that whole end of innocence thing. Or maybe that Jones, unlike so many big names today, seemed to really enjoy being a pop star while never acting as if it was a birthright."[15] Musician Richard Marx dedicated a lengthy blog post to the influence Jones gave him as a child. "Davy Jones was, aside from Elvis, my boyhood hero. I loved The Monkees, yes … but it was all about Davy. He was so cool. His clothes, his moves, his voice, and he ALWAYS got the girl. I wanted to meet Davy more than anything." As it happens, Marx's father had a connection to a local radio station and was able to arrange a meeting. "You know that thing about meeting your heroes and how it can often be a total letdown? This was the polar opposite. The radio guy brought me into another room at the station and there sat Davy Jones, alone. He was only about 5'4" but when he stood up he seemed 6'6". He was handsome and had this big smile on his face. This was one of the most famous people on the planet and it was just me and him. He'd been told I was a big fan (how unique!) and he asked me lots of questions about myself and my family and what I liked at school, etc. Davy sat and talked to me for about 15 minutes. He drew a picture on a piece of paper and signed it for me, and put his arm around me as I left, giving me a hug." The most telling line in Marx's story is, "He couldn't have been more who I wanted him to be in that moment." Marx recalls meeting Jones at an airport later in life and having Jones compliment his own music, treating him like a colleague and no longer merely a fan. "And he said he still loved to perform. He said, 'We've just got to keep doing it, right, man? It's who we are.'"[16] Of note in an increasingly tag-lined, search-engine-lead internet life, is that once Marx connected his name to *The Monkees*, ads for his upcoming albums appeared before episodes of *The Monkees* posted to YouTube.

The depth of loss and seriousness of the reaction to Jones' death brought a new urgency to attendance at the reunion concerts that Nesmith finally rejoined and in a ripple effect, brought critics to take the performances more seriously. It also brought an outpouring of love from Jones' many fans, enough that they contributed financially to the support of his stable full of rescue horses, creating a club called Davy's Angels.[17] How often does fan support follow a teen idol beyond the length of their mortal life?

The Musician/True Hippie—Peter

Peter Tork underwent perhaps the deepest changes from who he was before being cast in the show, who he became during *and* after, and how he eventually earned respect for his virtuoso musicianship in the later round of reunion tours where he began to play a wide variety of instruments—along with bits of Bach concertos between songs. Discovered as a young performer just out of Greenwich Village, he had the least connection to Hollywood, yet the part required the most acting talent. In early teen magazine interviews his fellow actors clarified the difference between Tork and Peter the Monkee. "They all speak up as one about his acting ability. Davy says: "Mostly, on the television shows, we three are just playing ourselves. But Peter really has to play a part. You see, he's really very intelligent and he's also the quietest one of us four. So when he plays that way-out character in the TV series ... well, it's just not him at all! Those double-takes and the way he looks kinda baffled ... that's not our off-stage Peter!"[18] According to associate producer Ward Sylvester, the producers cast Peter to fill the type of role that the actor Huntz Hall filled in the Bowery Boys (in another Monkees/Beatles connection Hall was one of the celebrities on the cover of The Beatles' *Sgt. Pepper's Lonely Hearts Club Band* album). Such a character seems not quite stupid but he was "just kind of unsure of himself." Since Tork was quite well educated, he became the only actor playing a character far different from himself, and in many ways paid the price for that artistic choice.[19] Until the reunion tours reassessed his persona, the naïve klutz dogged Tork for years. In an appearance on *The David Letterman Show* in 1982, Tork tripped on his way to the desk for the sake of the laugh. In discussing the character he played, Tork summarized, "He was really stupid."

Once the other three characters were set, only Peter's persona required a choice, as mentioned by writer Treva Silverman in Chapter Three. It fell to the staff writers to decide if Peter would play a genius or a total idiot, largely based on where they could mine the most humor and idiot won the choice. The results of that decision came to fruition first in season one episode three "Monkee vs Machine"—as did the evidence of the original confusion. When the characters are two days late on the rent they peruse the classifieds for jobs. Discounting openings for lion tamers and piano delivery boys, Micky finds a position perfect for Peter: "Toy factory needs unskilled help in unessential job requiring no training and no experience." As the dialogue introduces Peter's naivete, the visual counters it because as they talk to Peter, he is playing chess. Clearly, the prop department had yet to get the memo on the writers' final choice between genius and idiot. While that visual denies Peter's 'idiocy,' the rest of the episode defines it. When Peter answers the ad, the interviewer turns out to be a computer, which confuses Peter's name, turning it from "Not what" to "Nit Wit." Peter becomes flustered and asks, "Why do I have to talk to a machine?

Why can't I talk to a human being?" This suggests the other aspect of Peter's personality that came from the actor more so than from the writers. Peter appeared to be the truest peacenik, or hippie, among the others. This comes through across the two seasons in points of view Peter takes and in the clothing—love beads and moccasins—that Tork brought to the character.

The naïve Peter appeared mostly in the first season, from signing a lifetime contract for dance lessons in "Dance, Monkees, Dance" to "Son of a Gypsy" where, when they tell him if the others don't bring back the Maltese Vulture soon it's "curtains for him," Peter responds, "Thank heaven. I thought you were going to kill me." A combination of his naïve nature and his dedication to his musicianship formed the basis for his being fooled into selling his soul to the Devil in order to learn to play the harp in "The Devil and Peter Tork." Seeds of the idea that Tork could play many instruments come from the fact that Peter played a variety of instruments across the episodes—from the bass guitar to the piano to the banjo (in the "Monkees on Tour" documentary episode) to the pipe organ to the harp.

Like Dolenz, Tork took his turn behind the camera for season two, episode 23 "Monkees Mind Their Manor" (written by Coslough Johnson) and, in terms of the use of names, for his directing credit Tork chose to use his real name, Peter H. Thorkelson, rather than his stage name. It is no surprise that when it was his chance to have a say in how to immortalize the character of Peter, Tork focused on Peter being a music maker. The episode opens with Peter leading rehearsal and asking his band mates to "see if you can pick this up," showing him to be the lead musician. It includes a comment that highlights his personal philosophy of social justice, "The problem is getting out of here keeping our consciences clear," and ends with Peter interrupting Mike's end-of-show speech by asking for time to give their Christmas message of Peace and Love. All his colleagues recognized Tork as the truest hippie of the group. During promotion for their film *Head*, Jones gave an interview to *16 Magazine* where he promised, "the movie is as different from the Monkees' TV series as day is from night.... Peter goes to war. I mean, can you picture peaceful Peter in a fox-hole?"[20]

Unlike Dolenz, who worked as a director after *The Monkees*, Tork never followed up on the opportunity. Rather he chose to return to his roots as a musician after the show was cancelled and he severed his ties with the band. Perhaps due to the controversy over studio musicians play-ing on the band's first two albums it took years for music critics to recog-nize Tork's musical abilities. A typical review of their 2014 reunion tour brought out comments such as: "Of the original three, Peter Tork moves around and pulls pranks most like his young self, but his quiet musician-ship is fun to watch as he jumps from instrument to instrument, especially when he pulls the banjo out."[21]

Finally, while countless polls taken by teen magazines almost always ranked Davy and Micky among the audience favorites, Peter had his fans as well. From colleague and writer Treva Silverman, who chose him as her favorite, to modern times when musician, columnist, and avowed life-time fan, Dempsey Gibson, recalled meeting Tork at a club as "One of the best days of my life."[22]

The Songwriter/Father Figure—Mike

Whether it was due to his being older (than Dolenz and Jones but not Tork), or due to his being tall, or because he was already a father in real life, Mike did provide the father figure from the start. The program provided the fantasy of a father-knows-best-less house, but because of Mike they had a father figure. Over time Nesmith also became synony-mous with songwriting, rebellion against other authority and (true or not) being an actor trapped in a character he had come to detest.

Mike's father-figure persona is apparent in the pilot. As Davy is preparing for his date with Vanessa, Mike asks him where he is going, then adds, "Might rain. Better take your galoshes." In a fake, hick accent and a fatherly tone Mike finishes with, "Please, son, don't talk to no strangers after midnight." Later in the episode when Davy walks off upset and Peter attempts to follow him, it is Mike who says, "He's uptight. Just let him go" and Peter obeys. Even later, Mike functions as the therapist to Davy who needs to find a way to help Vanessa. Later, in the fantasy sequence where they declare a board meeting to handle the problem, it is Mike who sits at the head of the table, brandishing the gavel. In "Monkee vs. Machine," Mike gets the upper hand on the fancy new HR computer.

In "Success Story" it is Mike who approaches Davy's grandfather and accuses him of wanting Davy to return to England only to make himself happier, not for Davy's own good. When Davy does leave, Mike admonishes him to "be good." In "I Was a Teenage Monster" Mike refuses to help the evil doctor by teaching his Frankensteinian monster to play rock and roll. "Doctor, I cannot risk the lives of myself and my men for such a foolhardy experiment." In "Devil and Peter Tork" Mike's defense of Peter saves the day, followed by his telling Peter to go play the harp and prove he's always had the power and the talent. Beyond words, visuals often illustrate where the leadership fell, for instance in "Monstrous Monkee Mash" Peter lays his head on Mike's shoulder, safe there with the father figure. Likewise Micky, while walking down the hall toward danger, hides behind Mike though they are essentially the same height. Nesmith carried the paternal place in the band into their later years. In 1996 when the foursome had come back together and released *Justus*, an album of new music, and announced a new tour, Nesmith came to the defense of his bandmates when the album received some negative critical reception. After defending songs written by his other colleagues, Nesmith questioned the grammar behind the old insult regarding playing their own instruments, "And by the way, what do you mean, or does anybody mean for that matter, 'play their own instruments'? Whose instruments do you suggest we play? Or is this just a parroted phrase, whose garbled meaning only bothers serious writers?" He followed that comment up with the promise to, "keep my eyes open for the review that understands the music as it was intended and offers real and, I am hopeful, constructive comments on how it may have been better. Yours is not it. Instead, it seems to me, it's half-witted journalism, combined with poor writing skills and even less insight."[23]

In other episodes, Mike is defined as a songwriter, something audience members would have learned if they watched the credits of the program each week and often saw Nesmith's name connected to songs such as "Papa Gene's Blues," "Mary, Mary" and "The Girl I Knew Somewhere." In "I've Got a Little Song Here" (written by Treva Silverman) the Mike character receives a letter offering to purchase his songs. Davy asks, "You wrote a song?" Mike admits he has and then Peter announces, "Hey, Mike's a songwriter," identifying him fictionally one of the ways he functioned for the group in reality. When the group teases him, Mike tells them to go on laughing, "songwriting is a million dollar business," which for Nesmith, it was. Jones would often speak in later interviews about how Nesmith never needed to go on reunion tours because he made more money than any of them by making sure his own tunes were the B sides to the group's major hits. The other show moment that solidified Mike as a serious songwriter came when Frank Zappa guested on the show, dressed as Mike and Mike appeared dressed as Zappa. The approval of such an alternative rock performer added gravitas to Mike's standing as a songwriter. They discuss the differences between the music of the Mothers of Invention and the Monkees and Zappa, speaking as Mike, says when the show is over he plans to join the Byrds. The idea that he could move into one of the most innovative and successful new bands speaks to the general idea that Nesmith was the leader of The Monkees, expected to go on in music rather than as an actor once the show ended. During the later reunion tours, though Nesmith declined to join in as a performer, the others chose to sing some of his songs ("Mary, Mary," "Listen to the Band") as a method of inclusion. In his role as emcee at these concerts, Dolenz often listed the great songwriters the Monkees were given and always included Nesmith. In fact, in his solo musical tours Dolenz often made time for his sister, a member of the back up band, to do a solo of Nesmith's "Different Drum."

Nesmith's Texas roots also meant his character covered that stereotype. Ward Sylvester defined it as a "Will Rogers kind of country and western figure."[24] Hence titles like "Hillbilly Honeymoon," which involved Mike's country cousins in a Hatfield and McCoy kind of feud and comic lines such as in "Monkees at the Circus," when they all identify as brain surgeons, Mike adds: "Except in the summer when I'm a cotton picker." Then he begins giving the Farm Report, which became a standard improvised piece they performed during radio station visits while promoting their concert tours. At the end of "Monstrous Monkee Mash" Mike and Micky improv by asking each other what their groovy buttons say. Micky's says "Love is the Ultimate Trip" and Mike breaks down in giggles several times before being able to admit his button says "Save the Texas Prairie Chicken."

The later reputation Nesmith received for rebelling against authority came from his push for the actors to have a say in the music they recorded, which has been nicknamed the 'palace revolt' and resulted in the ouster of music supervisor Don Kirshner. Somehow the unrest Nesmith felt over the music situation blended into a common notion that he also detested the character he played. Though he denied this in countless interviews, the idea resonated in the Hollywood community so much so that in 1999 the film *Galaxy Quest* included a character named Jason Nesmith. A parody of actors caught in the personas of their long ago canceled sci-fi-fantasy show attending a *Star Trek* style convention to make a living, the

Jason Nesmith character is clearly based on William Shatner and Leonard Nimoy. Yet Nesmith is the name writers David Howard and Robert Gordon chose for that character. Was it because it was reminiscent of another actor who was known to have become resentful about his part on a popular program because he felt it caused a crimp in the rest of his career?

When his future bands did not reach similar levels of fame as the Monkees and Nesmith turned to producing music and films, he became the leader he had played on both seasons of the program. The resentful reputation followed him through the early reunion tours when he only stepped in for a concert or two, but never for a full summer tour. Though he did not participate in the 1986 concert tour, Nesmith attended the concert at Arlington Stadium in Texas in 1986 and gave an interviewer his impression of the band and on the fandom. "I got some inkling of what the whole thing was about. I wondered to myself if I could have ever been a Monkees fan, because I really liked that experience; I liked the way Micky sang, I liked the way Davy sang and the way he looked. I liked the love that was exchanged between the audience and the performers, and the reciprocity of it, which was complete. There was a lot coming off the stage from those guys, and a lot going back to the people. It was edifying on one hand, but on the other hand it was uplifting. I had never realized that that was going on at Monkees concerts because what I was trying to do was play loud enough so I could be heard."[25]

Still, the question of his unhappiness constantly came up in interviews once he did fully rejoin the tours of 2012–2014. When asked if the Monkees (both the television program and band) was something he was happy to have been a part of, Nesmith replied, "Very happy with the Monkees as an early part of my career. It was fun and a great way to spend my 20s. I loved it."[26] That became a talking point, as is clear from this similar response to yet another interview that year, "Never did my love for the Monkees, and my love for Micky and Peter and Davy, diminish. It was fun, it was great. I had it as part of my life."[27] Lest it be thought that these are responses carved solely in the wake of Jones' death, Nesmith responded in a similar way in a 1994 appearance on *Later with Greg Kinnear* (himself a huge fan). For Kinnear, Nesmith defined his time on the show as, "very good" and used the Italian word "amarcord." Also the name of a Federico Fellini movie, Nesmith defined amarcord as the idea of a way to "color the past so you remember the good stuff. We tend not to remember the pain." He even defined Micky as his favorite Monkee in the interview.

Yet for all his public clarification of how he felt, interviewers continue to ask Nesmith if he hated his time on the show—or any of his fellow actors. His rejoining the reunion tours after Jones' death caused those questions to resurface. The VH1 film *Daydream Believers* further entrenched Nesmith into both the leader and father figure persona and the myth of hating the experience as the dramatic arc of the script revolves around his coming to appreciate what *The Monkees* meant. After dramatizing many known events (the auditions, the backlash of the press, the controversy over who did and did not play their own instruments, etc.) the television film ends with the Jones character coming to visit the Phyllis Nesmith character in the hospital after a car crash (itself as fictionalization in that she had once experienced a major car crash but never entered the hospital for care as she was a Christian Scientist). *The Monkees* has been cancelled at this point in the film but the mother of a young fan comes to ask the Jones character to visit her daughter in the room next door, which he does. Then another young fan with a broken arm in a cast approaches the Nesmith character and asks, "You're a Monkee, too, aren't you?" To which the Nesmith character says, "Yeah, yeah, I guess I am a Monkee" which illustrates his acceptance as the over-arching theme of the film. In the ending scene, the Nesmith character describes the looks on the faces of these children as 'magical' and the Dolenz character describes it as "Monkee magic" and declares "It's not really such a terrible way to make a living if you think about it" and the Nesmith character asks "Now why didn't anybody tell me *that* two years ago?"

In his comments on one of Nesmith's 2014 solo performances, Joe Valle, the music columnist for philly2philly.com, encompasses both the old and the new concept about Nesmith:

> While Nesmith sometimes gets a bad rap for being labelled the "serious" Monkee, he came off as sincere, humorous, introspective and gracious throughout the night and hasn't really lost much of his vocal range at 70 years of age. Whether he's conscious of the effect the Monkees have had on multiple generations is unknown (a massive security guard prevented us from talking to him), but the ear to ear smile after the thunderous ovation he received by the audience isn't something you can fake. The inclusion of another well-known Monkees song would've been the icing on the cake, but Michael Nesmith has always been a man who's stayed true to himself and his convictions.[28]

Fans who focused on Mike as their favorite Monkee, and Nesmith as their favorite musician in the band, have defended him with similar words across the years. Clearly, his talent as a songwriter and his authenticity shined through any manufactured controversies created by the media.

The Monkees (as a Whole)

While the fictional version of Nesmith's coming around in *Daydream Believers* is exactly that, fictional, it was also magical, as evidenced by his actual return to touring with Dolenz and Tork post Jones' death. Music critics and longtime fans came out of the woodwork where they had long been hiding their obsession. They offered praise and analysis that further defined the identity of the group as a whole, such as this one by PopDose blogger Allision Johnelle Boron in her "Why This Monkees Tour Matters" post:

> Unexpected, heart-wrenching and spirit-lifting. I'm not one to cry at concerts, especially with bands I've seen many times, but I couldn't help it losing it a little. The sheer surprise of hearing his voice deliver a piece of Davy that is near-holy relic status is what officially stamped this performance as The Best Monkees Concert Ever(tm).
>
> Nez singing a verse of "Daydream Believer" has surely happened before; in fact, a version of him on lead vocals exists. But on this tour, in this context, it is a cathartic experience. Where the 2012 tour was dubbed the unofficial "Davy Jones Memorial Tour," this one is more about healing, acceptance, and the future. For me, and many fans, I'm sure, it proved a certain peace within the fold.
>
> The poignancy of the gesture is simple, but meaningful. Recognition from one polarized heavyweight to another, with a simple message: "You will never be forgotten and you will always be one of us."
>
> And that's why this tour is so great—for that one, shining moment at the very end of the concert, the Monkees are whole again.[29]

Dan Moore of the Phoenix New Times, who interviewed Dolenz about the success of the reunion tours wrote, "the one thing Dolenz won't tell you, while he's telling you everything else about the Monkees—at least not explicitly—is just how much of it depended on the band itself, and their uncanny ability to sell "Daydream Believer" and improvised pratfalls in the same half-hour." Moore went on to claim their success was definitely a blend of both the acting and the performing and further credits The Monkees for creating a brand of their own, one that has yet to be matched. "The Monkees' odd formula—too much a band to just be musical comedians, too much a troupe of musical comedians to just be a band—made their shifting reputation inevitable, but their staying power means they're now a formula of their own. Shows like *Glee* and *Big Time Rush* try for the same combination of surreality and precise pop earnestness, even if they rarely end up tapping into the weird anarchy that drove John Lennon to compare the Monkees to the Marx Brothers." Moore summarizes this chapter best when he writes, "Of course, his [Dolenz] self-interview is its own testament to the intuitive grasp the Monkees have on their half-fictional selves. It's its own reminder that after 40-plus years—no matter how and why they came together—Micky Dolenz, Peter Tork, and Michael Nesmith are very good at being the Monkees."[30]

Ten

What Am I Doing Hangin' Round?
The Cultural Cachet
of *The Monkees*

The Monkees' cultural cachet refers to the influence they had over the music, other television programs, and even the politics of their day and beyond, though it took nearly 50 years for mainstream critics to finally recognize that cachet. *The Monkees* influenced the culture of their time, but manufactured controversy transformed them into a guilty pleasure for fans at best and worthy of ridicule at worst. No doubt the continued concert reunions of Jones, Dolenz and Tork kept the fans fed and eventually won over critics, who finally began giving them fair and positive reviews in their 2011 tour. Then, Jones died in 2012, leading to a rapid wholesale rehabilitation of their reputation in the higher levels of pop culture, gratifying from a personal standpoint and fascinating to watch as a scholar. The evolving meanings popular culture has made of *The Monkees* and their music over the past 50 years is a journey from Kellogg's cereal and Nerf commercials to the *Brady Bunch* to *Breaking Bad* to the *Porsche Macan*. Part baby boomer nostalgia and part something deeper and more complex has been at work.

The original cultural cachet involved a Hirschfield drawing made of them for *TV Guide* in 1966 and Davy's guest appearance on *The Brady Bunch* in 1971, two seasons after the show's cancellation (the most re-run episode of television ever according to his obituary on *CBS Sunday Morning*). When the show descended into the Saturday morning cartoon schedule, they very nearly disappeared from the small screen for twenty years. Then MTV ran their marathon weekend in 1986, the reunion concert tour reignited the flames of fandom, and it all faded back again until *Boy Meets*

World created a mini-reunion of Micky, Peter and Davy in 1994. Other intermittent moments happened on television such as Micky's voice was heard serenading "The Last Ever Seinfeld" with a parody of "Last Train to Clarksville" in 1998.[1]

Then, in the year Jones died, the critically acclaimed, hard-edged AMC drama *Breaking Bad* used Micky's vocals on the song "Goin' Down" for a montage of Walter White making meth in his makeshift lab. That exposure began a new run of references on several critically acclaimed television programs. In 2014 the Emmy-winning television program, *Mad Men,* set in the advertising world of the 1960s, used "The Porpoise Song" for the closing of their sixth season finale episode, "The Quality of Mercy." That same year a television commercial for the Porsche Macan[2] used "I'm a Believer" as their background music. For the series finale of *Glee* (which aired on the Fox Network on March 8, 2015) two main characters shared the song "Daydream Believer." That summer the Disney Company released another nature documentary based on the world of monkeys, *Monkey Kingdom,* which began with Dolenz' vocals on the classic theme song with a new verse. Shortly thereafter Netflix debuted *Grace and Frankie*, a new sitcom starring Jane Fonda and Lily Tomlin about divorced friends in their seventies. At the end of episode 11, *Secrets* (written by Nancy Fichman and Jennifer Hoppe), the two swap deep secrets about their teen years in the nineteen sixties. Tomlin's character tells Fonda's character that she once made out with a Monkee and it was Micky Dolenz. The show fades out on Dolenz' recording of "She" while Fonda's character responds by calling him, "The worst one." Considering Dolenz had the second highest amount of fan mail, this seems a mistake, though because the Fonda character is very overly concerned with looks perhaps the writers thought her character would not have found him cute enough. In truth, since Tomlin is playing an aging hippie, she ought to have made out with Peter Tork, but then that would involve the writers on the show having done deeper research into each actor's life. Still, the fact that Tomlin mentioned a Monkee rather than a Beatle insinuates that the Monkees' status was high in the 1960s, and regained its standing by the year of its 50th anniversary. Likewise, in the anniversary year Universal Pictures premiered *Minions*, a prequel to their *Despicable Me* franchise in which the charming, pill-shaped yellow characters sang many songs of the sixties including the theme from *The Monkees*. The newly revived concert tours sparked the Figures Toy Company to issue a set of action figures of the four band members. Perhaps the ultimate karmic result of years of rejuvenating their image comes from the fact that if you choose "Monkees" as a music form on iTunes radio, their songs will be accompanied by selections from such venerated groups as the Beach Boys, the Byrds, and the Beatles.

A final note on the long tail of their cultural footprint comes from the fact that the financial success of the show funded the filmmaking careers of show creators Bert Schneider and Bob Rafelson. Screen Gems executive Steve Blauner adamantly believed, "There'd have been no *Easy Rider* without *The Monkees* so they should canonize *The Monkees* just for that."[3] Though this book most concerns the television show, mention must be made of the film *Head* which, as Dolenz remembers it, had a theme of deconstruction. "Deconstruction of the Monkees certainly, but also the deconstruction of the Hollywood system. And they [the producers] did it. They singlehandedly created the independent film industry."[4]

Similar to a modern college course, the Monkees were transdisciplinary in that they were the first to captivate fans in two mediums, the television industry and the music industry, that each wing of show business normally kept separate. By succeeding in both those realms simultaneously *The Monkees* struck a chord in a much larger audience. But breadth of audience cannot account for their continued impact across five decades. Timing comes into consideration. Coming as it did in the midst of the birth of the 'young generation' they sung about, *The Monkees* became a part of their generational memory. In the 1920s, Hungarian sociologist Karl Mannheim articulated the theory that groupings of people are defined as generations by experiencing a noteworthy historical event while coming of age. Though he died just before the birth of the 1960s, Mannheim essentially predicted the rising of the social consciousness of the Hippie generation based on their experiencing the Civil Rights and anti-war movements and the nearly back-to-back deaths of Martin Luther King, Jr., President John Fitzgerald Kennedy, Malcolm X and Senator Robert Kennedy. Sociologists who came after Mannheim claimed the educated youth of the 1960s, watching the movements on television, learned more about the inequalities of American society than the generations that had come before them. They saw the success of the individual and collective action against those inequalities and chose to participate in such action across their lifetimes. The music of their youth became the score for those experiences. As it followed them through life this music served to remind them of that period when they felt the most empowered.

Proof of how deeply *The Monkees* connected to generational memory is nowhere more evident than in the transcripts of KDWB radio coverage of their arrival at the Twin Cities airport for a concert in Minnesota in 1967.[5] The interviews with fans waiting at the airport were interspersed with news reports of the near Civil War in Mainland China, a murder in San Francisco's hippie district, the fact that this had been the heaviest one day assault in the Vietnam conflict, and the fact that more troop build-up in Vietnam would mean continued draft calls that fall. While this radio show encapsulated the major political issues of the late 1960s, John Bodnar studied the effect of sharing the more personal issues of an era in "Generational Memory in an American Town." In his study of the baby boomer generation for *The Journal of Interdisciplinary History,* Bodnar defined them also by "their commitment to new sexual norms, their flight from marriage, and their experimentation with drugs and new musical forms."[6] Bodnar reports that most scholars who study baby boomers discovered a tendency to rebel against traditional institutions as a hallmark of its collective identity. That collective identity turned the boomers into an extended family unit, making continued visits with their distant cousins, *The Monkees,* a part of the family ritual created by these fans. Originally, these fans gained little respect because they were not the hippie generation; they were the preteen siblings of the hippie generation. According to Phil Gallo, *Billboard*'s senior correspondent, "The Monkees were the first group they could claim as their own, as opposed to the music that belonged to their parents. That really affects people."[7] With that in mind, it is possible to view their connection to *The Monkees* as something above and beyond a memory of music intertwined with the pathos of their era. They missed joining their older siblings, who were tuning in and turning on, so the preteen audience was drawn to *The Monkees* even more strongly because *The Monkees* were sharing the secrets of the '60s with those who were too young to yet live them. Then, by breaking up their musical collaboration shortly after the cancellation of their television program, the band became a symbol for the unfulfilled dreams and goals of their fans' generation, making their reunion tours, beginning in 1986 and continuing in every decade after, particularly poignant.

First off, to refute the cultural myth that all their peers reviled them in their first incarnation, it appears the opposite was the more true from the very beginning. As a television program, *The Monkees* won two Emmy Awards in their first season, for Outstanding Comedy Series and for Outstanding Directorial Achievement for a Comedy. In the Series category they beat the longer-running *The Andy Griffith Show* (1960–1968), *Bewitched* (1964–1972), *Hogan's Heroes* (1965–1971) and *Get Smart* (1965–1970). In the Directing category James Frawley won the vote of his peers over directors of the shows *Bewitched, I Spy, Family Affair* and *The Lucy Show*. Each category was a first win for the show and for Frawley it was the first and only win of three more nominations across his career. He also earned nominations for *The Monkees* in 1968 (when he lost to Bruce Bilson of *Get Smart*), *Ally McBeal* in 1997, and *Ed* in 2000.

Also, Frank Zappa was willing to appear as a guest in the episode "Monkees Blow Their Minds" (written by Peter Meyerson). If the other musicians of their day dismissed the program why would Zappa have risked association with it? Likewise, folk singer Tim Buckley appeared at the end of "Frodis Caper" to sing "Song to the Siren," a serious folk ballad, not a comic novelty song. According to several interviews Peter Tork gave over the years, his friend Janis Joplin had agreed to appear in season three, but the program was cancelled. Likewise, Tork brought friend Stephen Stills in to the studio to play guitar on one of the songs he wrote for the *Headquarters* album, "Long Title: Do I Have to Do This All Over Again?" That friendship also brought The Buffalo Springfield frontman, Neil Young, into the studio band fold. He played guitar on "As We Go Along," on "Smile," a backing track for the never completed "That's What It's Like Loving You," and on "the simply incredible 'You And I' which appeared on the underrated *Instant Replay* album in 1969."[8] Additionally, conductor and composer Quincy Jones chose to use instrumental versions of "I'm a Believer" and "She Hangs Out" in *Cactus Flower* (1969), the latter as the song Ingrid Bergman danced to alongside Goldie Hawn in what became Hawn's Academy Award-winning role in the film. Even after the show's cancellation the trend-setting composer still found the music respectable—as did later musicians of note.

So it seems the actual band and its members were not reviled so much as the hoopla surrounding them, as commemorated in the release of the Byrds song "So You Want to Be a Rock 'n' Roll Star" in 1967. Written by Jim McGuinn and Chris Hillman, the song did not lambaste the actual Monkees or their music, but focused more on the media craze that followed.

Nesmith reacted to the corporate control of their music in an interview after the cancellation of the program when he expressed the idea that the music establishment might have been jealous of their immediate success and denied them recognition as musicians. "People think we're tools of the establishment," he says, "but we're not. We're really the truest expression of the iconoclastic youth of today." In a prescient moment he said that with time that would change and they would be appreciated.[9] Nesmith could not have guessed it would take fifty years for his prediction to come true, but it did.

Despite whatever controversy they created in their own time, their influence carried across time and across mediums. It is widely known that David Bowie's birth name is, in fact, David Jones and he had to change it due to Jones' international popularity. It is equally recognized that the guitarist for U2, Edge, loves "Daydream Believer" and had Jones join him onstage in the Los Angeles stop of the 1997 U2 PopMart tour to sing the song to the packed concert hall. Likewise, on the radio program *Breakfast with the Beatles* Tork referenced the idea that Axl Rose of Guns N' Roses "stole" his very particular sideways dance moves from Davy Jones.[10] While that might sound like a compliment from a friend and colleague, it was repeated by Lyndsey Parker, managing editor of Yahoo! Music who said in an obituary for Jones, "I don't think you can overstate his influence. Even to the point where the first time I saw [Guns N' Roses lead singer] Axl Rose do that sideways shimmy of his, I thought, 'OK, he got that from Davy.'"[11] Along with already active artists, many nascent singer-songwriters trace their entrance into the music business to their introduction to both *The Monkees* and the Monkees. In 1994 Michael Stipe, lead singer of R.E.M. told *Rolling Stone* magazine that "the Monkees … meant a lot more to me" than the Beatles. He had reportedly vowed to bar R.E.M. from the Rock and Roll Hall of Fame until the museum inducted the Monkees, though in 2007 R.E.M. accepted their invitation to be inducted.[12]

In 1996 in a televised interview for the movie *Evita*, Madonna noted that the only difference between her and Evita Peron was that Madonna had a crush on a Monkee (Micky).[13] Similarly, in a 2014 interview Richard Shindell was asked about his earliest musical influences and immediately cited the Monkees: "My first favorite song was 'Daydream Believer,' the Monkees' version. How's that for guilty pleasure? I loved that song when I was 8 or 9 years old and I still love it."[14] Laura Cantrell echoed that point regarding a question about the first album she bought: "I was probably in about 5th or 6th grade and I went and bought a Monkees LP. The Monkees were not on television then but they were in repeats so I was quite excited to find that Monkees record and to buy it with my own money in the local record store when I was about 10 or 11 … it was actually their 'Greatest Hits.'"[15] When asked to name some favorite tracks, singer Annie Lennox chose "I'm a Believer" and wrote on her Facebook page, "It was written by Neil Diamond and recorded by the band, with lead vocals by Micky Dolenz. The single went to number 1 in the US chart on December 31 1966 and stayed there for seven weeks. The Monkees were a pretty great television boy band actually!"[16] While being interviewed on an episode of *The Katie Couric Show* guest Richard Marx shared his childhood love of the Monkees with a nearly blushing host. Then they discussed their deep feeling of loss after Jones died. Marx had written a long article about his personal connection to the Monkees on his blog, recorded himself singing "I Wanna Be Free," and posted it on YouTube.com in tribute to Jones.[17]

On the blog Marx wrote, "It was the winter of 1968 and aside from the Beatles, nothing on earth was bigger than The Monkees. In my house, however, The Monkees were everything. I didn't really catch up to how life-changing The Beatles were until later. I think I knew the words to 'Daydream Believer' and 'I'm Not Your Steppin' Stone' before I could speak in complete sentences. I … freaking … LOVED … The Monkees. I watched their show on TV every Saturday and begged my parents to buy me every record. One Christmas I even got the Matchbox car version of the Monkeemobile." Marx so loved the group a family friend who did radio promotion invited the young boy to meet them at his radio station where he met Jones, Dolenz and Nesmith. [He would meet Jones again as colleagues later in life.] Marx credits the Monkees with teaching him he could be a performer when he grew up: "I was in my first grade class and it was 'Show and Tell' time. The teacher called on me even though I wasn't volunteering, and I said I didn't have anything for her. She said, 'Your parents told me that you like to sing. Will you sing a song for the class?' I didn't want to, but my legs somehow got my body to the front of the group, and everyone got quiet. I was brutally nervous and wasn't even sure what to do. And then I just went with the one song I knew by heart: 'I Want To Be Free' by The Monkees, sung by Davy Jones."[18]

In concert in the 1990s the lead singer of Sawyer Brown introduced their country take on "Last Train to Clarksville" and blatantly admitted the band's musical influence came from the Monkees. According to songwriter Alee Willis, when Bright/Kauffman/Crane Productions hired her to help them write the TV show theme song for their new pilot, *Friends*, in 1994, they asked her to "write something Monkees-ish." Willis was more than happy to comply: "The Last Train to Clarksville definitely pulled into the station during those sessions."[19] In 2014 critics identified this same Monkees influence in the songs in *Up Here*, written by married songwriters Robert and Kristin-Anderson Lopez, who won the Academy Award for the main song in *Frozen* earlier that year.[20] Jazz vocalist Cassandra Wilson chose to end her sets with "Last Train to Clarksville" which Wilson, "now 58 and old enough to have witnessed the Monkees firsthand, recorded in 1996. Although harmonica fueled the proceedings, this wasn't a chugga-chugga train song. Rather, this fast train to rumblesville rambled along like a spaced out blues."[21] Of note also appearing in that music review was the critic's choice of ranking the Monkees as part of an essential set of the four M's "Bob Marley, Van Morrison, Joni Mitchell and the Monkees." In 2013 Tom Petty of Tom Petty and the Heartbreakers liked to open concerts with a double dose of Monkee-themed material by playing the Byrds' 1967 classic "So You Want to Be a Rock 'n' Roll Star" back to back with "(I'm Not Your) Stepping Stone."[22]

It could not be as damaging to reputation as has been reported to have loved the Monkees as many serious actors and others have had no qualms about mentioning such a feeling during interviews for their own upcoming projects. On *The Rosie O'Donnell Show* (01/21/97) actor Kevin Bacon spoke of his early love of music and stated that his heroes growing up were The Monkees, The Beatles, Bobby Sherman and David Cassidy. Even tennis star Andy Murray recalled The Monkees as a "musical touchstone" of his childhood. "My mum used to drive us a lot to and from tournaments that were five, six hours away, and singing was one way of keeping us amused."[23]

The parade of artists only grew in 1986 when MTV chose to air a marathon of reruns of *The Monkees* in honor of the 20th anniversary. A February weekend dubbed Pleasant Valley Sunday introduced a new generation to the program and therefore to the music. That reintroduction lead to a reunion tour for Dolenz, Jones and Tork which became one of the top ten financially successful concert tours of the summer, this time with pop culture icon Weird Al Yankovic as their opening act (rather than Jimi Hendrix). This incarnation of the band toured again several times across the decades. In 1996 all four original members reunited to create a new album, *Justus*, and a tour of the UK, but their cultural cachet experienced a deeper rebirth in the aftermath of Davy Jones' death in 2012, which also resulted in Nesmith finally fully joining a couple of reunion tours with Dolenz and Tork. The loss of one member and return of another brought other fans back into the fold, including magician and comedian Penn Jillette who openly declared his preteen love of *The Monkees* in a column for CNN. "I flew across the country to Philly to see them on stage. I had promised my 12-year-old self that I would see them live and I wanted to keep that promise. I owe the Monkees a lot. The Monkees got me started on crazy-ass rock 'n' roll and probably got me started doing my crazy Vegas magic show." Jillette credits *The Monkees* television program with introducing him to Jimi Hendrix and Frank Zappa and getting "the feeling and beat out there to the children," something for which he remained thankful. "And some of us, after feeling the beat and digging the feeling, kept going all the way, far out. The Monkees were an entry to rock 'n' roll as rebellious as it could get."[24] With their name continuing to come up in interviews with ground breaking new bands each decade, the Monkees stayed in the cultural consciousness. On *That Metal Show* Rob Zombie said if could play in any other band than his own, he would want to be in The Monkees.[25] The same Metal show noted that Kurt Cobain of Nirvana was a Monkees fan, too. Likewise, Lars Ullrich of Metallica is a Monkees fan and often discusses how he studied *HEAD* while preparing his own band film in 2013. In concert, Susanna Hoffs of The Bangles often comments that the Monkees were a big influence on her work.

The television aspect of *The Monkees* certainly made a difference between the way they and other rock bands of the time experienced their cultural connections. Many straight rock and roll bands of the day hit a peak during production of their original records. Once the radio airplay ended, they faded, only to return as novelty nostalgia acts such as Flo and Eddie of The Turtles in their "Happy Together" tours. Yet critics of the Monkees 2013 and 2014 concert tours found them still vibrant. "Some bands playing nostalgia concerts sometimes sound like a shell of their former selves. Yet The Monkees are all hovering around age 70 and sounded like younger musicians—especially Dolenz."[26] The Monkees (as a rock band) had the continued presence of their television program in perpetual reruns from Saturday mornings in the '70s through the MTV reruns of the '80s through Antenna Television using them as a foundation for their rise as a digital broadcast channel in the 2010s. Perhaps the biggest compliment to the program came when it was included in the lineup of the IFC (Independent Film Channel) in 2015. Executives at IFC announced the show belonged on their channel because its producers used the proceeds to fund the independent film movement of the 1960s. All these events made *The Monkees* culturally important enough to be included in CNN's coverage of television in their 10 part series *The Sixties* which aired in June and July of 2014.

As to the television of their own time, rumors of *The Monkees* having an effect on *Star Trek* continue to be debated on internet myth-checking sites that question the authenticity of a memo from Gene Rodenberry to that effect. According to historian Peg Lamphier, "Rumors are all about Popular Culture knowledge. The mere existence of such a rumor is proof of the importance of *The Monkees*. What the writers intended for *The Monkees* isn't always what the audience reads. The same is true of the writers of *Star Trek*. Whether they meant it or not, the audience reads Chekhov as Davy Jones which suggests the importance of the influence of *The Monkees*."[27] While it would be acceptable to end with that theory, a personal interview with *Trek* writer D. C. Fontana put an end to the mystery. According to Koenig, "Gene, in one of his memorandums, was quoted as saying he wanted to find someone who would have the same appeal as that little guy on The Monkees. That's about all I know." According to Fontana, "It was The Beatles that started it all. Maybe Gene just hitched onto the newest thing to 'sell' Desilu on the idea."[28] Worth noting is the fact that both programs aired on NBC, making early knowledge of the impact of Davy's popularity available to producers of their other programs.

The Monkees also influenced the existence and success of *Rowan and Martin's Laugh-In* first because the comedy variety show hosted by Dan Rowan and Dick Martin premiered after a first run episode of *The Monkees*, thereby providing the young audience the new show needed to be considered hip. Also two writers from *The Monkees* later joined the Emmy-winning staff of *Laugh-In*, David Panich and Coslough Johnson. In February of 1969 Jones appeared as a guest working in a sketch with JoAnne Worley and in October of that year Dolenz, Nesmith and Jones appeared to promote their newly formed trio, appearing in sketches as the musicians in the patriotic "Spirit of '76" painting (by Archibald Willard) and later in the program as knights from medieval times, reminiscent of the "Fairy Tale" episode.

Across the years many other television programs have found ways to homage *The Monkees*. In 1995 *The Ben Stiller Show* aired a sketch called

"The Grungies" which focused on a Seattle grunge band living their lives in visually similar circumstances as *The Monkees* only ... grungier. As the band prepares to play for a talent scout, a double-whammy of cultural cache occurred. During that episode, Pizza Hut aired their then new campaign with Ringo Starr announcing his desire to "get the other lads to agree" to get back together, but somehow the wrong lads show up. Rather than The Beatles, it's Micky, Davy and Peter who arrive to start eating their pizza crust first, though none of them are named, suggesting advertising executives who wrote the ad expected the audience to know who they were. Then "The Grungies" continues with part two involving the arrival of the talent scout, Josh Goldsilver, played by guest star Micky Dolenz. The writing staff of *The Ben Stiller Show* included future screenwriters such as Judd Apatow, Bob Odenkirk and Bruce Kirschbaum, as well as star Ben Stiller, and this sketch illustrates the influence *The Monkees* had in all their artistic endeavors.

In the late 1980s *Spitting Image*, the British puppet show that satirized politics and popular culture (often in a mean-spirited way), created the Mankees, a send up of *The Monkees* if they had never grown up and out of their pad. In 1997 *Muppets Tonight* aired another sketch about a band, this one called The Benedictine Monkees, a blend of The Monkees and The Benedictine Monks, famous for recordings of their Gregorian chants. On the show they performed as part of "Lollapalosers," a show full of performers not polished enough to be accepted to Lollapalooza, the annual music festival of alternative rock, metal, punk and hip hop bands. Sadly, this sketch still represented the band as losers despite the way the trend was turning. One of the cultural touchstones of the past 20 years, *The Simpsons*, saw fit to homage *The Monkees* twice. The first time involved a flashback to Marge's elementary school days. She carried a *Monkees* lunchbox onto the school bus only to be confronted by a bully who announced that they "don't even play their own instruments," yet again stirring that old controversy and lending it credence in the newer generation. The second *Simpsons* reference to *The Monkees*, fell in the 2014 season of the show concurrent with the band's third reunion tour post Jones' death. The character of Sideshow Bob (voiced by Kelsey Grammar) shows a slide with a chart explaining "Monkeys Saved vs. Brain Cells Lost" followed by a slide announcing "Research Funded by Mike Nesmith and Mick[e]y Dolenz."

Between reruns and homages, other chances to catch up with the cast came from the fact that they were actors as well. Even though Micky Dolenz spent more than a decade directing English television, he was also frequently called to do cameos for American filmmakers who had once been his preteen audience. For instance, director Rob Zombie was such a fan that he hired Dolenz to do a cameo role in his 2007 remake of *Halloween*.[29] Before that time, though, Dolenz had been seen acting on *My Three Sons* (1972), *Boy Meets World* (1994) and singing as himself on *Muppets Tonight* in the 1990s. He also maintained a steady career in cartoon voice overs so fans listened to him on everything from *The Tick* to *The Powerpuff Girls*.

Meanwhile, Jones had started the cameo portion of his career on the aforementioned *Brady Bunch* episode, an television event remembered by Lyndsey Parker, managing editor of Yahoo! Music, who said the day she saw the episode where Jones visits the Bradys "my head almost exploded."[30] Though other celebrities eventually guest starred on the show such as Desi Arnaz, Jr., Joe Namath and Don Ho, when *The Real Live Brady Bunch Stage Show* toured nearly three decades later (1994) it was the "Getting Davy Jones" episode that they spoofed by inviting Jones on the tour. Likewise, producers of the film spoof, made in 1995, deemed his appearance necessary for keeping the spirit of the show alive. From that original *Brady Bunch* episode he moved to *Love, American Style* and *My Two Dads* and *Boy Meets World* until the writers of Nickelodeon's highly successful *SpongeBob Square Pants* decided to play the ever-obvious name game, giving *Monkee* Davy Jones his own undersea locker on an episode in 2009.

On the flip side, neither Tork nor Nesmith cared much for acting once the show was over, appearing in only a handful of television programs. Tork shunned acting for years, so his appearances were nil until the nineties with *Boy Meets World* and *Seventh Heaven*. Nesmith stayed behind the cameras except for hosting the shows he produced, *Elephant Parts* and *Television Parts* (directed by Dolenz) in the early '80s. Perhaps his renewed interest in performing on tour starting in 2012 lead to a renewed interest in acting as in 2014 he accepted a guest starring role on a show with the hipster credentials of *Portlandia*, where he played the father of the city mayor and the secret money behind most of the city budget.[31]

Finally, in terms of influencing the politics of their day, the actors were admonished early on not to make public comments about anything controversial, particularly the war in Vietnam. In fact, according to several interviews with Dolenz across the years, they were told to make jokes if asked at all and play up their zaniness. Yet their mere existence on television had political overtones. Tork often refers to the lack of adult supervision seen in the lives of the fictional band and others invoke the idea that merely showcasing a group of long-haired hippies in a family time slot served to make them more palatable to the parents of real-life baby boomers. But there are other ways in which the program involved their teen audience in politics in the years before they could yet vote. For a large portion of the female audience the news that Davy Jones received his draft notice caused heightened interest in the Vietnam War and the intricacies of the Selective Service, interests that would only grow stronger as the boys in their own friendship circles soon became 18—and eligible.[32] Some girls from fan clubs in the UK organized protests where they marched in front of the American Embassy in London with posters reading "Don't Draft Davy."[33]

On a side branch of Monkee influence, songwriters Tommy Boyce and Bobby Hart lead a protest called LUV = Let Us Vote. The protest urged the United States Congress to pass a 26th amendment to the U.S. Constitution moving the legal age for voting from 21 to 18. During the 1960s, student activists protesting the Vietnam War began to argue that if men could be drafted to fight at 18 they should be able to vote for the political leaders who would send them to war. Boyce and Hart wrote the patriotically tinged song "L.U.V." that became the official campaign song for the movement.[34] While invoking the movement's theme the song also makes a nod to the hippie philosophy of non-violence with its lyrics.

Clearly *The Monkees* made contributions across culture, both nationally and internationally, in their 50 years of existence. Their continued clout comes from their having had feet in both the television and music industries at key changing points in each. Like Mickey Rooney and Tony Bennett, they kept at it long enough to work through the fallow periods and live long enough to finally be appreciated by all those pre-teeny-bopping fans who finally grew up still watching their beloved *Monkees*.

Chapter Notes

Introduction

1. Sotomayor, *My Beloved World.*
2. Mario Tarradell, "Nostalgia Packs a Powerful Punch During "Headquarters' Heavy Monkees Concert at Verizon Theater," *Dallas Morning News*, August 3, 2013. Retrieved from www.dallasnews.com.

Chapter One

1. Palladino, *Teenagers*, 52.
2. "Plastic Hippies Turn Strip into Nightmare," *Sarasota Journal.*
3. Eric Lefcowitz, *Monkee Business: The Revolutionary Made-for-TV Band* (New York: Retrofuture, 2010), 61.
4. Bodroghkozy, *Groove Tube,* 66–67.
5. Stempel, *Storytellers to the Nation,* 67–68.
6. *Ibid.*
7. Tobler, *NME Rock 'N' Roll Years*, 60.

Chapter Two

1. Gray, "The Time Seems Right for Judy Gold."
2. Moser, "Peter Tork at Peace with Post-Monkees Career."
3. http://www.examiner.com/article/author-monkees-were-countercultural-pioneers-as-much-as-the-beatles.
4. See Dolenz with Bego, *I'm a Believer: My Life of Monkees, Music, and Madness.*
5. Marcus, "The Monkees Still Have Plenty to Say."
6. Leary, *The Politics of Ecstasy*, 173–175.
7. http://blogs.mcall.com/lehigh valleymusic/2012/06/monkeeing-around-with-peter-tork-60s-tv-bands-bassist-talks-about-legacy-and-future-.html.
8. Weatherford, "The Monkees Prove Their Staying Power with Latest Tour," *Las Vegas Review-Journal,* August 9, 2013. http://www.reviewjournal.com/entertainment/music/monkees-prove-their-staying-power-latest-tour
9. Friedensen, "The Monkees' Raleigh Concert Will Cover Songbook, Tribute to Davy Jones."
10. Welch, "Hey, Hey They Wrote *The Monkees.*"
11. *Ibid.*
12. http://www.urbandictionary.com/define.php?term=Psycho%20Jello.
13. Buddha first taught the invocation of the phrase to a small group at Seicho-ji temple in Awa province, Japan, on April 28, 1253.
14. Silverman, *You Can't Air That.*
15. Bledsoe, "McGuinn's Influence Lingers On."
16. Carlin, "America the Beautiful."
17. Welch, "Hey, Hey They Wrote *The Monkees.*"
18. Personal interview with the author.
19. Sandoval, *The Monkees*, 81.
20. *Ibid.*, 123.
21. https://vault.fbi.gov/themonkees/The%20Monkees%20Part%2001%20of%2001/view.
22. http://blogs.villagevoice.com/music/2015/05/ed_sheeran_forest_hills.php.
23. Werts, "Tribute: Davy Jones and the Monkees Change the World."

24. http://www.examiner.com/article/ bob-dylan-s-influence-on-the-monkees? cid=taboola_inbound.

25. Maddow, *The Rachel Maddow Show.*

Chapter Three

1. Norman, *What Happens Next: A History of American Screenwriting* (New York: Three Rivers, 2007), 360–365.

2. Corliss, *The Hollywood Screenwriters*, 19–29.

3. Cavell, *Pursuits of Hollywood*, 8.

4. Welch, "Hey, Hey They Wrote *The Monkees.*"

5. *Ibid.*

6. *Ibid.*

7. Caruso died in 2012 and therefore could not be interviewed for this project.

8. Welch, "Hey, Hey They Wrote *The Monkees.*"

9. *Ibid.*

10. *Ibid.*

11. *Ibid.*

12. *Ibid.*

13. Schlitt died in 2008.

14. Welch, "Hey, Hey They Wrote *The Monkees.*"

15. *Ibid.*

Chapter Four

1. From 1961 to 1966 Rose Marie co-starred on *The Dick Van Dyke Show* as Sally Rogers, the single female comedy writer for the fictional *Alan Brady Show* alongside Buddy Rogers and Dick Van Dyke.

2. Pemberton, "The Monkees' Davy Jones Recalls Beatles Friendship and Mike Nesmith's Disloyalty."

3. Todd, "Hey, Hey We're the Wrinklies."

4. Krolokke, *Gender Communication Theories and Analyses: From Silence to Performance*, 20.

5. National Center for Education Statistics.

6. Of note is the fact that Queenie was played by Corinne Cole, who appeared as the Playboy Playmate of the Month in May 1958 under the pseudonym Lari Laine. It is highly unlikely young fans of the day knew that. What they would have made of it, we can only speculate. But it seems Cole was on the cusp of the move many former adult actresses and models (including Tracy Lord) would make, moving from the adult world into more mainstream entertainment. Does that make Cole a feminist role model or not?

7. Tong, *Feminist Thought: A More Comprehensive Introduction,* 3d ed., 284–285.

8. Wilson, 2012. "Bechdel Rule Still Applies."

9. http://stuartshea.blogspot.com/2010/ 02/phyllis-barbour-nesmith-rip.html.

Chapter Five

1. For a discussion of connections between Italian Americans and African Americans see Chapter 9, "Skin: Giancarlo and the Border Patrol," in Thomas J. Ferraro's *Feeling Italian: The Art of Ethnicity in America* (New York: New York University Press, 2005).

2. Gauthreaux, "An Inhospitable Land: Anti-Italian Sentiment and Violence in Louisiana, 1891–1924." University of New Orleans Theses and Dissertations. Paper 515. http://scholarworks.uno.edu/cgi/view content.cgi?article=1515&context=td.

3. Ferraro, *Feeling Italian,* 178–80.

4. Inge, *Charles M. Schulz: Conversations,* 256.

5. For more on the careers of Tim Reid and Tom Dreesen see: Tim Reid, Tom Dreesen and Ron Rapaport, *Tim and Tom: An American Comedy in Black and White* (Chicago: University Of Chicago Press, 2008).

6. "Comedians: They Have Overcome," *Time,* February 5, 1965, retrieved November 19, 2010.

7. The Maltese Vulture is a comedic homage to the Maltese falcon, made famous in *The Maltese Falcon* (1941) adapted for the screen by John Huston from the

Dashiell Hammett novel. The film starred Humphrey Bogart, whose other movie posters hung on the walls of the Monkees' pad.

8. Rock music scholars may note that a parking lot would appear in the lyrics of Joni Mitchell's "Big Yellow Taxi" three years later.

9. Linden had previous credits on *The Count of Monte Cristo*, starring Micky's father, George Dolenz.

10. Variously credited to Bob Dylan, Abbie Hoffman and Jerry Rubin, but correctly stated by Jack Weinberger according to several sources including the personal interview: "Don't Trust Anyone Over 30, Unless it's Jack Weinberg."

Chapter Six

1. Sandoval, *The Monkees,* 72.

2. Lewis, "'Davy Jones Deserves a Lot of Credit': Monkees Co-Creator Bob Rafelson."

3. https://www.youtube.com/watch?v=QXLvVx1EAx0.

4. Several books discuss the false story, but *The Simpsons* immortalized the fake moment in "Krusty Gets Kancelled" (original air date May 13, 1993), thereby cementing it in modern popular memory.

5. On May 9, 1961, Minow referred to television as a vast wasteland in his first address as chairman of President John F. Kennedy's Federal Communications Commission.

Chapter Seven

1. Oral history, Steve Blauner, http://www.youtube.com/watch?v=SYz-LRFhUWw&feature=related.

2. Franen began film editing in 1947 and moved into television in 1950. He came to *The Monkees* having earned one Emmy nomination in 1956 for *The Bob Cummings Show* and would earn another in 1974 for *Kojak*, which demonstrates the quality of talent drafted onto *The Monkees*.

3. Sandoval, *The Monkees*.

4. Iverson, *The Advent of the Laugh Track*.

5. *E! True Hollywood Story*.

6. Ashman, "I Make the Monkees Clothes."

7. Author interview with Dick Rawlings.

8. Kazmierczak, "The Monkees Dance on This Week."

Chapter Eight

1. Welch, "Hey, Hey They Wrote *The Monkees*."

2. http://www.monkeesconcerts.com/1/post/2014/03/headquarters-radio-program-interviews-ward-sylvester-part-2.html.

Chapter Nine

1. Kazmierczak, "The Monkees Dance on This Week."

2. Sandoval, *The Monkees*.

3. Kleiner,"Monkees Aren't Moaning about TV Setback."

4. http://www.monkeesconcerts.com/1/post/2014/03/headquarters-radio-program-interviews-ward-sylvester-part-1.html, at 37:50.

5. Benner, "Micky's Many Hairstyles."

6. http://www.thisdayinmusic.com/pages/daydream_believers,

Posted May 11, 2013, 18:44.

7. http://www.dailymail.co.uk/femail/article-2109014/My-love-affair-Davy-LIZ-JONES-recalls-childhood-obsession-Monkee-perfect-man-live-him.html#ixzz3515dKjuh .

8. http://www.youtube.com/watch?v=XFX5FLfaCbw.

9. http://www.axs.com/from-circus-boy-to-singing-monkee-micky-dolenz-endures-over-the-decade-13947.

10. http://blogs.mcall.com/lehighvalleymusic/2014/05/micky-dolenz-says-the-monkees-were-just-a-role-for-him-but-a-role-of-his-life.html.

11. http://somethingelsereviews.com/2014/06/04/one-of-the-best-pieces-ive-

done-just-how-did-micky-dolenz-end-up-working-with-rob-zombie/.

12. Guarino, "Micky Dolenz Revisits the Monkees," Chicago Sun-Times, May 28, 2014. Retrieved from www.mark-guarino.com.

13. Goldberg, "Why We Grieve Teen Idols: A Tribute to Davy Jones."

14. http://archive.freep.com/article/20120304/COL01/203040474/Mitch-Albom-Davy-Jones-was-a-Monkee-and-true-teen-idol.

15. Albom, "Davy Jones Was a Monkee and True Teen Idol."

16. http://richardmarx.com/2012/02/richard-marx–vlog-davy-jones-february-29–2012/.

17. Salk, "Davy Jones Fans Return Love, Support His Horses."

18. http://monkees.coolcherrycream.com/articles/1967/06/monkees-monthly/peter-tork-the-talented-monkee.php.

19. http://www.monkeesconcerts.com/1/post/2014/03/headquarters-radio-program-interviews-ward-sylvester-part-1.html.

20. Stavers, "The Monkees and You."

21. http://www.detroitnews.com/article/20140531/ENT04/305310028#ixzz33Jyq61TQ.

22. http://www.salisburypost.com/article/20140413/SP01/140419880/1016/winek-a-column-gibson-hopes-his-quirky-television-series-finds-a-big-time-home.

23. http://www.monkees.net/this-is-now-nesmith-comments-on-justus-reviews/.

24. http://www.monkeesconcerts.com/1/post/2014/03/headquarters-radio-program-interviews-ward-sylvester-part-1.html, at 37:5558:11.

25. http://www.monkees.net/tour-1986–20th-anniversary-north-american-tour/.

26. http://www.amny.com/entertainment/q-a-with-monkee-michael-nesmith-1.7370167.

27. http://somethingelsereviews.com/2014/04/09/never-did-my-love-diminish-michael-nesmith-on-his-emotional-return-to-the-monkees/.

28. Vallee, "Michael Nesmith of the Monkees Delights Fans at Phoenixville's Colonial Theatre."

29. http://popdose.com/5-reasons-why-this-monkees-tour-matters/.

30. http://www.phoenixnewtimes.com/music/musical-comedys-latest-revival-owes-a-lot-to-the-monkees-6459465.

Chapter Ten

1. Monkees Micky Dolenz sings about the last episode of Seinfeld, http://www.youtube.com/watch?NR=1&v=8NUs_vZre7o

2. http://www.autoevolution.com/news/porsche-macan-commercial-believer-video-79000.html.

3. Oral history, Steve Blauner, http://www.youtube.com/watch?v=SYz-LRFhUWw&feature=related.

4. http://voices.suntimes.com/arts-entertainment/the-daily-sizzle/micky-dolenz-revisits-the-monkees-current-reunion-looks-back-at-60s-pop-heyday/#.U4zYNJSwKKx.

5. http://www.radiotapes.com/KDWB/KDWB-AM_Monkees_1_8–3–1967.mp3.

6. Bodnar, "Generational Memory in an American Town."

7. Goldberg, "Why We Grieve Teen Idols: A Tribute to Davy Jones."

8. http://dangerousminds.net/comments/when_neil_young_met_the_monkees_and_completely_tore_the_roof_off_the_sucker.

9. Kleiner, "Monkees Aren't Moaning About TV Setback."

10. Peter Tork on Breakfast with the Beatles, June 16, 2013. http://beatlesradioshows.tumblr.com/post/53138298417/http-www-divshare-com-direct-24220323–11b-mp3

11. Currie, "How to Help Horses Helped by a Monkee."

12. Dionisio, "Rock Hall Snub Irks Ex-Monkee."

13. http://www.monkees101.com/poptvfaq.html.

14. http://www.eagletribune.com/local/x1387846649/Musical-influences-the-mysteries-of-songwriting-and-God.

15. http://www.exeterexpressandecho.co.uk/Singer-Laura-Cantrell-reveals-musical-tastes/story-20538168-detail/story.html#ixzz2sTyq4uGI.

16. http://aberdeen.stv.tv/58968/.

17. https://www.youtube.com/watch?v=KZ5Mx0AH0OI#t=70.

18. *Ibid.*

19. http://www.alleewillis.com/blog/tag/monkees-merchandise/.

20. Fung, "Fresh Off 'Frozen.'"

21. "Cassandra Wilson Gives a 'Blue Light' Special Show at the Dakota," www.startribune.com.

22. Roberts, "Review: Deep Cuts from Tom Petty & the Heartbreakers at the Fonda."

23. Briggs, "French Open 2014."

24. Jillette, Penn. "Have Yourself a Merry Atheist Christmas!"

25. https://hardrockdaddy.wordpress.com/?s=rob+zombie.

26. Kaufman, "The Monkees Turn Back the Clock in Fun, Energetic Show."

27. Interview with P. Lamphier.

28. Interview with D. C. Fontana.

29. http://somethingelsereviews.com/2014/06/04/one-of-the-best-pieces-ive-done-just-how-did-micky-dolenz-end-up-working-with-rob-zombie/.

30. della Cava, "Davy Jones of the Monkees: A Towering Multimedia Star."

31. http://connect.oregonlive.com/staff/kturnqui/index.html.

32. http://monkees.coolcherrycream.com/articles/1967/07/teen-life/davy-jones-may-be-drafted.php.

33. http://frontporchnewstexas.com/df1967.htm.

34. *Time Magazine*, vol. 93, no. 5 (January 31, 1969): 20.

Bibliography

Ashman, Gene. "I Make the Monkees Clothes." *16 Magazine,* October 1967, 6–8.

Barker, Chris. *Making Sense of Critical Studies: Central Problems and Critical Debates.* London: Sage, 2002.

Barrett, Joel. "Musical Influences, the Mysteries of Songwriting and God." Retrieved from http://www.eagletribune.com/, March 6, 2014.

Benner, Ralph. "Micky's Many Hairstyles." *Tiger Beat Magazine,* January 1968, 12–15.

Bledsoe, Wayne. "McGuinn's Influence Lingers On." *St. Louis Post-Dispatch,* July 3, 1992, G4.

Bodnar, John. "Generational Memory in an American Town." *The Journal of Interdisciplinary History,* 26(4), (1996), 619–637. Retrieved from http://www.jstor.org/stable/205044.

Bodroghkozy, Aniko. *Groove Tube: Sixties Television and the Youth Rebellion.* Durham, NC: Duke University Press, 2001.

Braunstein, Harold (producer), and Neill Kearnley (director). *Daydream Believers: The Monkees' Story.* Canada: World International Network, 2000.

Brazis, Tamar, ed. *Thirty Years from the Home of Underground Rock: CBGB & OMFUG.* New York: Harry N. Abrams, 2005.

Briggs, Simon. "French Open 2014: Andy Murray Will Be Out to Erase Memory of Philipp Kohlschreiber Drubbing." *Telegraph,* May 30, 2014, accessed June 7, 2014, http://www.telegraph.co.uk/sport.

Bronson, Harold (producer), and Alan Boyd (director). *Hey, Hey We're the Monkees.* Discovery Channel, 1997.

Carlin, George. "America the Beautiful." On *Class Clown* [CD]. Los Angeles: Atlantic Records, 1972.

Cavell, Stanley. *Pursuits of Happiness: The Hollywood Comedy of Remarriage.* Cambridge: Harvard University Press, 1981.

Corliss, Richard, ed. *The Hollywood Screenwriters: A Film Comment Book.* New York: Avon, 1970.

Cosgrove, Ben. "The Invention of Teenagers: LIFE and the Triumph of Youth Culture." http://time.com/, September 28, 2013.

Currie, Carol McAlice, and Michael Davis. "How to Help Horses Helped by a Monkee." *Statesman Journal,* http://www.statesmanjournal.com, August 12, 2015.

della Cava, Marco. "Davy Jones of the Monkees: A Towering Multimedia Star." *USA Today,* http://usatoday30.usatoday.com/life/people/obit.

DiBlasi, Alex. "In Defense of the Monkees." *American Music Review,* XLI(2), Spring 2012. Retrieved from http://www.brooklyn.cuny.edu/web/academics/centers/hitchcock/publications/amr/v41–2/diblasi.php#8.

Dimock, Duane, and Sanford, Jay Allen. "Monkee Business." *San Diego Reader,* http://www.sandiegoreader.com/, September 10, 2008.

Dionisio, Joseph. "Rock Hall Snub Irks Ex-Monkee: Peter Tork Says Rolling Stone Editor Jann Wenner Is Blocking the Group's Induction to the Cleveland Museum." *Los Angeles Times,* http://articles.latimes.com/2007/may/04/entertainment/et-tork4, May 4, 2007.

Doherty, Thomas. *Teenagers and Teenpics: The Juvenilization of American Movies in the 1950s.* Philadelphia: Temple University Press, 2002.

Dolenz, Micky, with Mark Bego. *I'm a Believer: My Life of Monkees, Music, and Madness.* Lanham, MD: Cooper Square, updated 2004.

"Don't Trust Anyone Over 30, Unless It's Jack Weinberg." *The Berkeley Daily Planet,* http://www.berkeleydailyplanet.com/issue/2000-04-06/article/759, April 6, 2000.

Dullum, Daniel. "Review: Monkees' Appeal Spans Generations." *Florence Reminder & Blade Tribune,* http://www.trivalleycentral.com/florence_reminder_blade_tribune/news/review, August 15, 2013.

FBI. "The Monkees Part 01 of 01." https://vault.fbi.gov/the-monkees/The%20Monkees%20Part%2001%20of%2001/view.

Ferraro, Thomas J. *Feeling Italian: The Art of Ethnicity in America.* New York: New York University Press, 2005.

Friedensen, Roger. "The Monkees' Raleigh Concert Will Cover Songbook, Tribute to Davy Jones." Newsobserver.com, June 18, 2013.

Fung, Lisa. "Fresh Off 'Frozen,' Bobby Lopez and Kristen Anderson-Lopez Prepare a New Musical." *New York Times,* http://www.nytimes.com/, July 23, 2015.

Gibson, Phyllis (Nesmith). Obituary. *Los Angeles Times,* February 25, 2010. http://www.legacy.com/obituaries.

Goldberg, Stephanie. "Why We Grieve Teen Idols: A Tribute to Davy Jones." CNN, http://www.cnn.com, March 1, 2012.

Goostree, Laura. "'The Monkees' and the Deconstruction of Television Realism." *Journal of Popular Film & Television* 16(2), (1988), 50–58.

Gray, Margaret. "The Time Seems Right for Judy Gold." *Los Angeles Times,* June 6, 2013, D7.

Greenberg, Bradley, and Pilar Baptista Fernandez. *Mexican Americans: The New Minority on Television.* East Lansing: Michigan State University Press, 1979.

Hamill, Pete. *Why Sinatra Matters.* Boston: Little, Brown, 1998.

Harper, Janice. *Davy We Hardly Knew Ye: Why the Monkees Matter.* Huffington Post, http://www.huffingtonpost.com/, March 5, 2012.

Hewitt, Michael (producer), and Brian Henry Martin (director). *Making the Monkees.* Smithsonian Channel, 2007.

Hine, Thomas. *The Rise and Fall of the American Teenager.* New York: Avon, 1999.

Inge, M. Thomas. *Charles M. Schulz: Conversations.* Jackson: University Press of Mississippi, 2000.

Iverson, Paul R. *The Advent of the Laugh Track.* Hempstead, NY: Hofstra University Archives, 1994.

Jamieson, Patrick, and Daniel Romer. *The Changing Portrayal of Adolescents in the Media Since 1950.* New York: Oxford University Press, 2008.

Jillette, Penn. "Have Yourself a Merry Atheist Christmas!" CNN, http://www.cnn.com/, December 13, 2102.

Jones, Davy, with Alan Green. *They Made a Monkee Out of Me.* Beavertown, PA: Dome, 1987.

Kaufman, Doug. "The Monkees Turn Back the Clock in Fun, Energetic Show." *The Telegraph,* http://www.thetelegraph.com, June 9, 2014.

Kazmierczak, Russ, Jr. "The Monkees Dance on This Week." Nerdvana, http://blogs.evtrib.com/nerdvana/, August 4, 2013.

Keefe, Don. "Monkeemobile History from Pontiac Enthusiast Magazine." *Pontiac Enthusiast Magazine,* June 1, 2000. Retrieved from http://www.monkees.net/.

Kelley, John. "The Monkees: Still Monkeying Around and Inspiring Others to

Play Their Songs." *The Washington Post,* http://www.washingtonpost.com, July 19, 2013.

Kleiner, Dick. "Monkees Aren't Moaning about TV Setback." *The Phoenix,* March 1968, 21.

Krolokke, Charlotte, and Ann Scott Sorensen. *Gender Communication Theories and Analyses: From Silence to Performance.* Thousand Oaks, CA: Sage, 2005.

La Sorte, Michael. *La Merica: Images of Italian Greenhorn Experience.* Philadelphia: Temple University Press, 1985.

Leary, Timothy. *The Politics of Ecstasy.* Berkeley, CA: Ronin, 1998.

Lewis, Randy. "'Davy Jones Deserves a Lot of Credit': Monkees Co-Creator Bob Rafelson." *Los Angeles Times.* http://latimesblogs.latimes.com/music_blog, March 1, 2012.

Lewis, Richard Warren. "The Monkees: When Four Nice Boys Go Ape!" *The Saturday Evening Post,* January 28, 1967.

MacDonald, J. Fred. *Blacks and White TV: Afro-Americans in Television Since 1948.* Belmont, CA: Wadsworth, 1992.

Maddow, Rachel. *The Rachel Maddow Show,* http://www.nbcnews.com/id/263 15908/ns/msnbc_tv-rachel_maddow_show/#46610498, March 2, 2012.

Marcus, Jeff. "The Monkees Still Have Plenty to Say." *Goldmine: The Music Collector's Magazine,* January 25, 2012. Retrieved from http://www.goldmine mag.com/.

Martinez, Tomas. "How Advertisers Promote Racism." *Civil Rights Digest* (Fall 1969), 10.

Marx, Richard. "Davy Jones February 29, 2012." [Richard Marx VLOG]. Retrieved from http://richardmarx.com/2012/02/richard-marx-vlog-davy-jones-february-29-2012/.

McCracken, Grant. *Transformations: Identity Construction in Contemporary Culture.* Indianapolis: Indiana University Press, 2008.

Modderno, Craig. "Monkees Tour Pays Homage to Jones." *Music News,* http://

www.variety.com/article/VR1118065072/, January 24, 2013.

Moll, George (producer). *VH1 Behind the Music: The Monkees.* Gay Rosenthal Productions, 2000.

Moore, Dan. "Musical Comedy's Latest Revival Owes a Lot to the Monkees." *Phoenix New Times,* http://www.phoenixnewtimes.com/music/, August 8, 2013.

Moser, John J. "Peter Tork at Peace with Post-Monkees Career." *The Morning Call,* http://articles.mcall.com/, June 2, 2012.

National Center for Education Statistics. http://nces.ed.gov/programs/digest/d99/d99t187.asp.

Nefer, Barbara. "From Circus Boy to Singing Monkee, Micky Dolenz Endures Over the Decades." AXS, http://www.axs.com/ , July 7, 2014.

Palladino, G. *Teenagers: An American History.* New York: Basic, 1996.

Palmer, Jim. "We Took a Lot of Flak at the Outset': Peter Tork Talks to Vibe about The Monkees Returning to London." *The Wandsworth Guardian,* July 15, 2015. Retrieved from www.wandsworthguardian.co.uk/news/13419480.

Pemberton, Pat. "The Monkees' Davy Jones Recalls Beatles Friendship and Mike Nesmith's Disloyalty." July 13, 2011. Retrieved from Monkees.net.

"Plastic Hippies Turn Strip into Nightmare." *Sarasota Journal,* November 13, 1969, 20.

Press, Andrea L. *Women Watching Television: Gender, Class, and Generation in the American Television Experience.* Philadelphia: University of Pennsylvania Press, 1991.

Radio Tapes. August 8, 1967. Retrieved from http://www.radiotapes.com/KDWB/KDWB-AM_Monkees_1_8-3-1967.mp3.

Roberts, Randall. "Review: Deep Cuts from Tom Petty & the Heartbreakers at the Fonda." *Los Angeles Times,* http://www.latimes.com/, June 4, 2013.

Robinson, Mark (producer), and Gareth Williams (director). *We Love the Monkees.* United Kingdom: ITV Productions, 2012.

Bibliography

Ross, Sharon Marie, and Louisa Ellen Stein, eds. *Teen Television: Essays on Programming and Fandom.* Jefferson, NC: McFarland, 2008.

Salk, Susan. "Davy Jones Fans Return Love, Support His Horses." December 4, 2013. Retrieved from http://offtrackthoroughbreds.com/.

Sandoval, Andrew. *The Monkees: The Day to Day Story of the '60s TV Pop Sensation.* San Diego: Advantage, 2005.

Savage, Jon. *Teenage: The Creation of Youth Culture.* London: Viking/Penguin, 2007.

Schmich, Mary. "Yes, Peter Tork of the Monkees Can Play: Teen Idol at 71 Held the Stage with Flair." *Chicago Tribune,* http://articles.chicagotribune.com/, June 12, 2013.

Selbo, Jule. *Film Genre for the Screenwriter.* New York: Routledge, 2015.

Shipton, Alyn. *Nilsson: The Life of a Singer-Songwriter.* New York: Oxford University Press, 2013.

Silverman, David S. *You Can't Air That: Four Cases of Controversy and Censorship in American Television Programming.* Syracuse, NY: Syracuse University Press, 2007.

Spigel, Lynn, and Michael Curtin, eds. *The Revolution Wasn't Televised: Sixties Television and Social Conflict.* New York: Routledge, 1997.

Sotomayor, Sonya. *My Beloved World.* New York: Alfred A. Knopf, 2013.

Stavers, Gloria. "The Monkees and You." *16 Magazine,* June, 1968, 16–20.

Stempel, Tom. *Storytellers to the Nation: A History of American Television Writing.* New York: Continuum, 1992.

Sunshine Factory. http://monkees.coolcherrycream.com/articles/.

Sweeney, Gael. "The Face on the Lunch Box: Television's Construction of the Teen Idol." *Velvet Light Trap* (1994), 33, 49.

Sylvester, Ward. "Interview on *Headquarters Radio Show*: With Ward Sylvester (Part 2)." March 16, 1989. Retrieved from http://www.monkeesconcerts.com/.

Tobler, John. *NME Rock 'N' Roll Years.* London: Reed International, 1992.

Todd, Ben. "Hey, Hey We're the Wrinklies (The Monkees are back 45 years on... with a £1m motive)." MailOnline.com, http://www.dailymail.co.uk/tvshowbiz/, February 22, 2011.

Tong, Rosemarie. *Feminist Thought: A More Comprehensive Introduction,* 3d ed. Boulder, CO: Westview, 2009.

Valentino, Silas. "Ed Sheeran Helms the Modern British Invasion at Forest Hills Stadium." May 28, 2015. Retrieved from http://blogs.villagevoice.com/music/.

Vallee, Joe. "Michael Nesmith of the Monkees Delights Fans at Phoenixville's Colonial Theatre." November 10, 2013. Retrieved from http://www.philly2philly.com/.

Welch, Rosanne. "Hey, Hey They Wrote *The Monkees*: How the Writing Staff of *The Monkees* Helped Change the Face (or at Least the Hair-Length) of Television." *Written By Magazine* (December 2102), 46–52. http://www.mydigitalpublication.com/publication/?i=135356.

Werts, Diane. "Tribute: Davy Jones and the Monkees Change The World." TV Worth Watching, March 1, 2012. Retrieved from http://www.tvworthwatching.com/.

Whalen, Thomas J. "'I'm a Believer': Why the Monkees Deserve a Place in the Rock and Roll Hall Of Fame." April 30, 2015. Retrieved from http://cognoscenti.wbur.org.

Willis, Allee. "Allee Willis' Kitsch o' the Day: Talking Monkees Doll." [Allee Willis Blog]. August 12, 2009. http://www.alleewillis.com/blog/tag/monkees-merchandise/.

Wilson, Sarah. "Bechdel Rule Still Applies to Portrayals of Women in Films." *The Oklahoma Daily,* http://oudaily.com/news/2012/jun/28/bechdel-rule-col/, June 28, 2012. Accessed April 20, 2013.

Zilch: The Podcast Full of *The Monkees* Cast. http://zilchmonkeescast.blogspot.com/.

Index

Index

Index

Index